Windows 10 Anniversary Update Explored

Books by the Same Author

BP762	Microsoft Office 2016 Explained
BP757	Windows 10 Explained
BP747	Windows 8.1 Explained
BP743	Kindle Fire HDX Explained
BP741	Microsoft Office 2013 Explained
BP738	Google for the Older Generation
BP735	Windows 8 Explained
BP284	Programming in QuickBASIC
BP259	A Concise Introduction to UNIX
BP258	Learning to Program in C
BP250	Programming in Fortran 77

Books Written with Phil Oliver

BP726	Microsoft Excel 2010 Explained
BP719	Microsoft Office 2010 Explained
BP718	Windows 7 Explained
BP710	An Introduction to Windows Live Essentials
BP706	An Introduction to Windows 7
BP590	Microsoft Access 2007 Explained
BP585	Microsoft Excel 2007 Explained
BP584	Microsoft Word 2007 Explained
BP583	Microsoft Office 2007 Explained
BP569	Microsoft Works 8.0 & Works Suite 2006 Explained
BP563	Using Windows XP's Accessories
BP557	How Did I Do That ... in Windows XP
BP555	Using PDF Files
BP550	Advanced Guide to Windows XP
BP545	Paint Shop Pro 8 Explained
BP538	Windows XP for Beginners
BP525	Controlling Windows XP the Easy Way
BP514	Windows XP Explained
BP509	Microsoft Office XP Explained
BP498	Using Visual Basic
BP341	MS-DOS Explained

Windows 10 Anniversary Update Explored

by

N. Kantaris

Bernard Babani (publishing) Ltd
The Grampians
Shepherds Bush Road
London W6 7NF
England

www.babanibooks.com

Please Note

Although every care has been taken with the production of this book to ensure that all information is correct at the time of writing and that any projects, designs, modifications and/or programs, etc., contained herewith, operate in a correct and safe manner and also that any components specified are normally available in Great Britain, the Publishers and Author(s) do not accept responsibility in any way for the failure (including fault in design) of any project, design, modification or program to work correctly or to cause damage to any equipment that it may be connected to or used in conjunction with, or in respect of any other damage or injury that may be so caused, nor do the Publishers accept responsibility in any way for the failure to obtain specified components.

Notice is also given that if equipment that is still under warranty is modified in any way or used or connected with home-built equipment then that warranty may be void.

© 2017 BERNARD BABANI (publishing) LTD

First Published – January 2017

British Library Cataloguing in Publication Data:

A catalogue record for this book is available from the British Library

ISBN 978 0 85934 768 6

Cover Design by Gregor Arthur

Printed and bound in Great Britain for Bernard Babani (publishing) Ltd

About this Book

Windows 10 Anniversary Update Explored was written so that you can find out quickly what is new in Microsoft's major **Windows Anniversary OS** (Operating System) update.

It is assumed here that you already have **Windows 10** installed on your PC, but to find out which exact version of **Windows 10** you have, tap or left-click the **Start** button (the **Windows** icon on the extreme bottom-left of the screen), shown here, to open the screen in Fig. 1.

Fig. 1 The Left-click Windows 10 Menu Screen.

On the screen above, tap or click on **Settings** and on the displayed screen (shown on the next page), select **System**.

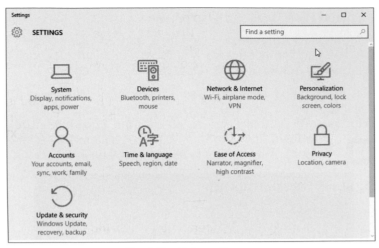

Fig. 2 The Settings Screen.

Next, tap or click **About** on the displayed menu (left of screen) to display what is shown on the right of Fig. 3 below.

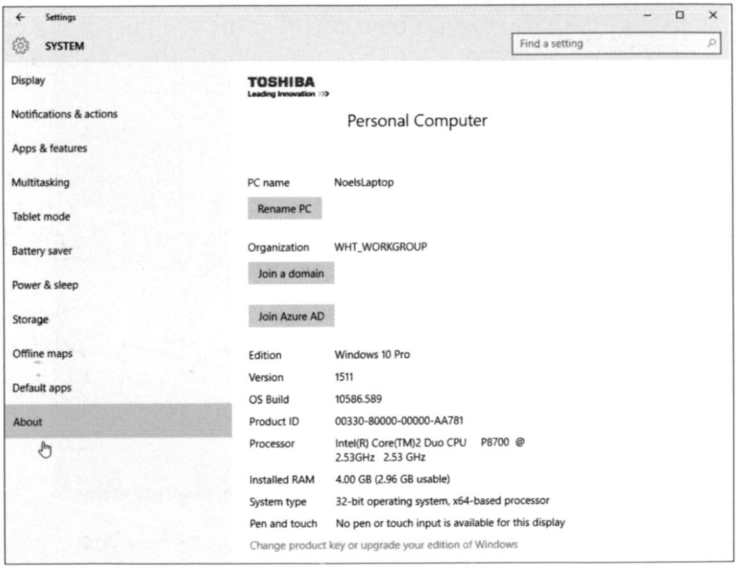

Fig. 3 The System Screen.

In the case of my Toshiba laptop, the version of **Windows** is displayed as **Windows 10 Pro** which indicates that this computer has not yet been updated to **Windows 10 Anniversary** – a totally free update to **Windows 10** as of the time of writing.

Another indication that this PC has not yet been updated is the fact that the buttons above the **Start** button (see Fig, 1 on page v) display with labels – more about this in the next chapter.

System Requirements

> **Note:** If your PC is already running **Windows 10**, it will also run the **Anniversary Update**.

To receive the **Anniversary Update** (as well as all future updates) turn on automatic updates by tapping or left-clicking the **Start** button, then selecting **Settings** and choosing **Update and Security** (see Fig. 2 on previous page) and turning **Automatic Updates** to **On**.

From here on you have two choices:

- Wait for the **Anniversary Update** to be downloaded by itself, which will save you at least half an hour before you are invited to install the update, but it might take several days before it happens, or

- Force a download manually by going to **Start**, **Settings**, **Update and Security**, **Check for Updates** to find the **Anniversary Update**. Make sure you have half an hour spare, as the download takes place in real time.

In this book, there are chapters that include the following:

- Installing the **Windows 10 Anniversary Update**

- The new **Start** menus and screens of the update and how to set **Active Hours** and other tweaks.

- **OneDrive** and printing **PDF** files.

- What is new in **Cortana** and how to use its settings.

- The **Taskbar** and **Actions Centre**.

- The **Microsoft Edge** browser.

- **Microsoft Ink**, **Dark Theme** and **Tablet** mode.

Note: In this book I only discuss the differences between **Windows 10** and the **Windows 10 Anniversary Update**. Therefore, I assume that you are familiar with **Windows 10** and you do not need to be told in detail how it and its apps work.

However, if you are new to **Windows 10**, then may I suggest that you have a look at my book *Windows 10 Explained* (9780 0 85934 757 0) also published by Bernard Babani (publishing) Ltd.

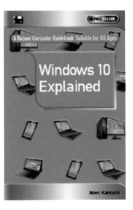

In this book, you will find details of how to update from an earlier version of **Windows**, as well as detailed understanding of **Windows 10**, its environment and how to use its various apps.

About the Author

Noel Kantaris graduated in Electrical Engineering at Bristol University and after spending three years in the Electronics Industry in London, took up a Tutorship in Physics at the University of Queensland. Research interests in Ionospheric Physics, led to the degrees of M.E. in Electronics and Ph.D. in Physics. On return to the UK, he took up a Post-Doctoral Research Fellowship in Radio Physics at the University of Leicester, and then a lecturing position in Engineering at the Camborne School of Mines, Cornwall, (part of Exeter University), where he was also the CSM Computing Manager. Later he also served as IT Director of FFC Ltd.

Trademarks

Microsoft, **Windows 10**, **Windows 10 Anniversary**, **Microsoft Word** and **Microsoft Print to PDF**, are either registered trademarks or trademarks of **Microsoft Corporation**.

Wi-Fi is a trademark of the **Wi-Fi Alliance**.

Adobe, **Adobe Acrobat** and **Adobe Reader** are either registered trademarks or trademarks of **Adobe Systems Incorporated**.

All other brand and product names used in the book are recognised as trademarks, or registered trademarks, of their respective companies.

Contents

1

The Anniversary Update

In this chapter I'll investigate what happens during and after the download of **Windows 10 Anniversary Update**.

Installing the Windows 10 Update

As discussed in the prelims, there are two ways of upgrading to **Windows 10 Anniversary**. One method is to wait for the **Windows 10 Anniversary Update** notification to appear (which was the case with one of my laptops), while the second is to force the download which is the method I chose for the other laptop and is the one I'll discuss here.

On attempting to download the update on this particular laptop, the screen in Fig. 1.1 was displayed.

Fig. 1.1 The Windows 10 Anniversary Update.

Obviously, there is some issue here with my printer (you might not have such a problem), so I clicked the **Fix issues** button to continue which then displayed the screen in Fig. 1.2.

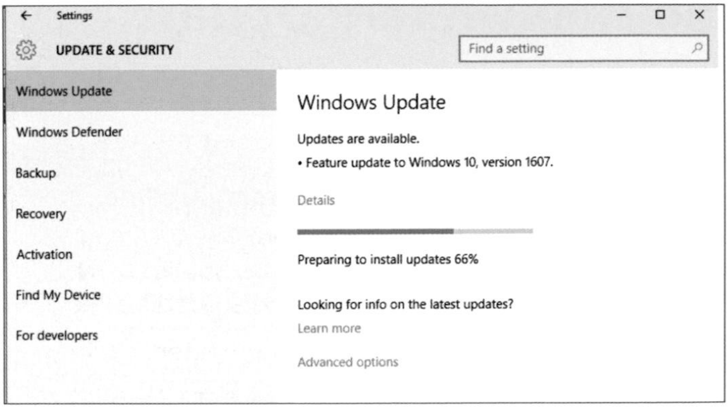

Fig. 1.2 The Windows 10 Anniversary Update Download.

The download of **Windows 10 Anniversary Update** took a good half hour, after which the computer displayed the screen in Fig. 1.3.

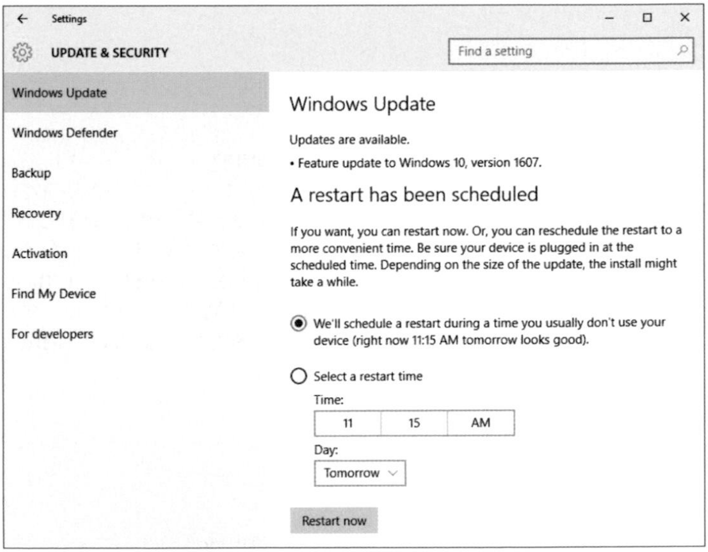

Fig. 1.3 Scheduling a Restart for the Installation of the Update.

As you can see, it is possible to schedule for a convenient time for the **Restart** which would then carry on the rest of the installation in your absence. Naturally, I wanted to see exactly what happens during that process, so I chose the **Restart now** option instead. You, of course, don't need to follow my example. Just schedule for a convenient time, but perhaps you might like to read what happens after this **Restart**.

After such a **Restart**, you are informed that "Windows is configuring the update and not to turn off your computer". This takes about 10 minutes, then the computer performs another **Restart** and another screen is displayed, this time saying "Working on Updates. This will take sometime". Now is a good time to put the kettle on and make a pot of coffee!

After a further 20 minutes, the computer performs yet another **Restart** and a further screen is displayed which says "Working on updates 30%. This will take a while", but this time it adds "Your PC will restart several times". When the process reaches 75%, the computer performs another **Restart**.

Depending on the speed of your computer's processor, what follows can take anything between 40 and 50 minutes to complete, after which you are greeted with the message "Hi. We have updated your PC. Getting things Ready. Please don't turn off your PC".

Further screens are displayed during that period with messages such as "These updates help protect you in an online work", "Go to **Start** and use the **Get Started** app to see what's new", "Making sure your apps are good to go" and finally, "Let's start", which displays a typical advertisement for **Windows Hello** devices, with part of the screen shown here in Fig. 1.4.

Windows Hello

Windows Hello changes how you think about passwords. Password-free sign-in gives you the fastest and most secure way to unlock your Windows devices.¹ Using your face, fingerprint or companion device, it recognises you – apart from anyone else. It'll wave you in with a friendly hello and even works on apps and Microsoft Edge websites.²

Shop Hello devices

Fig. 1.4 The Windows Hello Screen.

The Get Started App in the Update

To find out what is new in the **Windows 10 Anniversary Update**, click on the **Get Started** app, shown here, to open the screen displayed in Fig. 1.5.

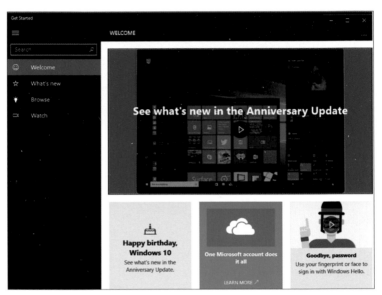

Fig. 1.5 The Welcome Screen of the Get Started Dialogue Box.

On the left of the above screen, you have a menu of three other choices. You can select to view **What's new**, **Browse topics** or **Watch videos**. Actually the **Welcome** and **What's new** menu options lead you to some brief overview videos telling you in general terms what new features are to be found in the **Windows 10 Anniversary Update**. Have a look for yourself!

One extremely useful screen is displayed when you choose the **Browse topics** menu entry, shown in Fig. 1.6 on the next page. Note that when such a screen is minimised, the words of the menu options are replaced by small images. Finally, the last menu option, **Watch videos**, displays a screen (part of which is shown in Fig. 1.7) with several informative videos.

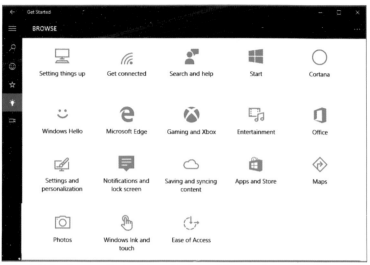

Fig. 1.6 The Browse Topics Menu Options of the Get Started Dialogue Box.

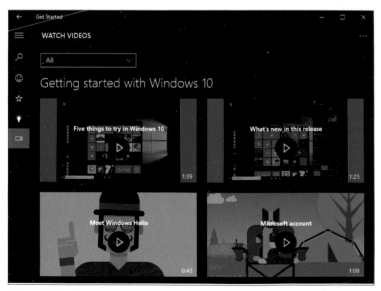

Fig. 1.7 The Watch Videos Menu Options of the Get Started Dialogue Box.

I suggest you spent some time watching these videos. Try it!

What Changed With the Anniversary Update

In short, what has changed with the **Windows 10 Anniversary Update** is as follows:

- Provided your computer has a fingerprint recognition pad or a face recognition camera, then you could use the **Windows Hello** app to sign into apps and Websites without having to use passwords.

- A slightly different **Start** menu – gone is the **All apps** option. Instead all your installed apps are listed on the left-side of the menu with added functionality.

- **Cortana**, the digital assistant which has been vastly improved to keep up with rivals from Apple and Google.

- A slightly different **Taskbar** menus and **System Tray** icons with the **Clock** and **Calendar** now combined and the ability to **Customise** both.

- Improved **Notifications** in the **Action Centre**. They are now grouped by app rather than displaying chronologically. You can even set priority levels within each app.

- The ability to set **Active Hours** (to correspond to your working hours on the computer), so that no updates can take place during that time. Gone is the frustration of having updates taking over your computer, when all you wanted to do is answer an e-mail.

- The Internet browser **Edge** now has added extensions and other improvements, making the **Internet Explorer** almost redundant, but still included in the update.

- The addition of more pen and stylus features with **Windows Ink**. These are similar to the features found in the **Edge** browser in **Windows 10**.

- The ability to change the display colour of some default **Windows** apps, dubbed the **Dark Theme**.

- Redesigned emojis which are now more detailed and expressive in appearance and also larger than before.

The changes listed so far, are not the only ones introduced with the **Windows 10 Anniversary Update**. Apart from specific capabilities, such as that of playing games purchased for the **Xbox** onto **Windows 10** devices and vice versa or use of the **Cortana** app for **Android** devices to allow **Notifications** to appear on both, there are a lot more changes not visible to the user which serve to make **Windows 10** more efficient and robust.

Most of the listed changes will be discussed in more detail in the next few chapters, but for now I need to correct the error that occurred during the download of the update, relating to my printer. You might have a similar problem!

Removing Previous Version of Windows

Windows keeps the previous version of its Operating System on disc, after upgrading, in case you need to roll back to it. However, this takes a lot of hard disc space, so if the new version works fine, you might want to regain the space that the previous version occupies on your hard disc.

To remove the previous version of **Windows 10** do this:

* Tap or left-click the **Start** button to reveal all your apps.

* Tap or click the **Settings** button pointed to in Fig, 1.8 .

Fig. 1.8 The Settings Button.

- This opens the **Settings** screen, shown in Fig. 1.9.

Fig. 1.9 The Settings Screen.

- Next tap or click the **System** option and on the displayed screen select **Storage** to display the screen in Fig. 1.10.

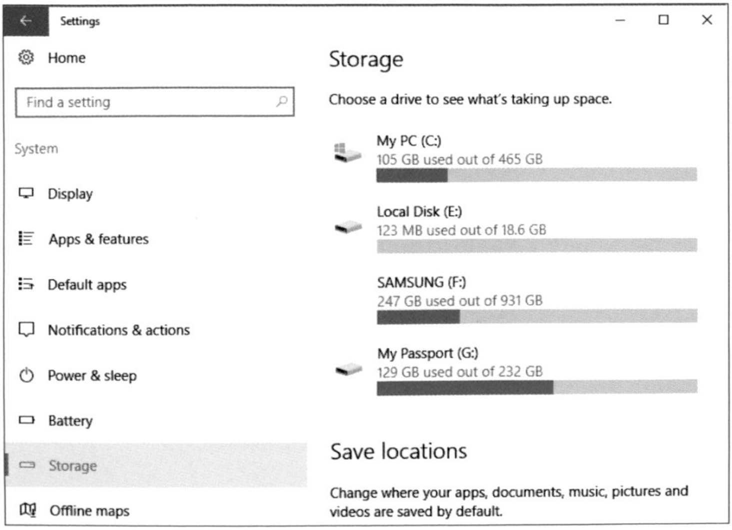

Fig. 1.10 The Storage Screen in Settings.

- Now tap or click the **My PC (C:)** entry at the top-right of the above screen, then scroll down to the **Temporary files** list of the displayed screen to open the screen shown in Fig. 1.11 below and select the **Previous version of Windows**, then tap or click the **Remove files** button.

As you can see in Fig. 1.11, this will reclaim 25.3 GB of disc space. Believe me it only takes a few taps or clicks to achieve this in a lot less time that it took to describe it, as discussed on the next page.

Fig. 1.11 Removing the Previous Version of Windows.

The short notation to get to Fig. 1.11 is: Go to **Start**, **Setting**, **System**, **Storage**, **My PC (C:)**, **Temporary files**. Just as I said, a few taps or clicks!

While you are on this topic, have a look in your **Downloads** folder to see if you can delete old downloaded files and save some more disc space. In my case there are 2.26 GB of files.

The Improved Windows Defender

Windows Defender with its anti-virus, anti-spyware and **Firewall** elements, can make your computer very secure with its protection working unobtrusively in the background. The improved **Windows Defender** also comes with the ability to use it as an additional defence against viruses, if you happen to be using another third-party anti-virus program. In the past, you had to choose between a third-party anti-virus program or **Windows Defender**.. You could not have both running

Now, if you have another anti-virus program installed, you could turn on the **Limited Periodic Scanning** option provided by **Windows Defender**, to act as an additional protection. To do so, go to **Settings**, **Update & security**, then select **Windows Defender** and turn on **Limited Periodic Scanning**. This does what it says; it periodically scans your computer and reports on the result, in addition to any scans offered by the third-party software

> **Note: Limited Periodic Scanning** only becomes available in **Windows Defender**, if you have installed third-party anti-virus software in which case you have to enable it yourself.

A few days after choosing **Windows Defender** to be my preferred anti-virus protector, the dialogue box shown in Fig. 1.12 on the next page, popped up on my screen.

Tapping or clicking on the **Turn on** button causes a further screen to be displayed, part of which is shown in Fig. 1.13.

Fig. 1.12 The What's New in Windows Defender Dialogue Box.

Fig. 1.13 Part of the Windows Defender Settings Screen.

As you can see, with **Windows Defender** you can have full protection at no extra cost. The **Windows Defender** app is in a sub-menu of the **Windows System**. To find it, go to **Start**, then scroll down to **Windows System**, then tap or click the down-arrowhead against it to open its sub-men. Next, tap and hold, or right-click its icon and select **Pin to Start**, so you can find it easier.

From then on, to find out whether your computer is protected, tap or click the **Windows Defender** icon on the **Start** menu, shown here, to display the screen in Fig. 1.14.

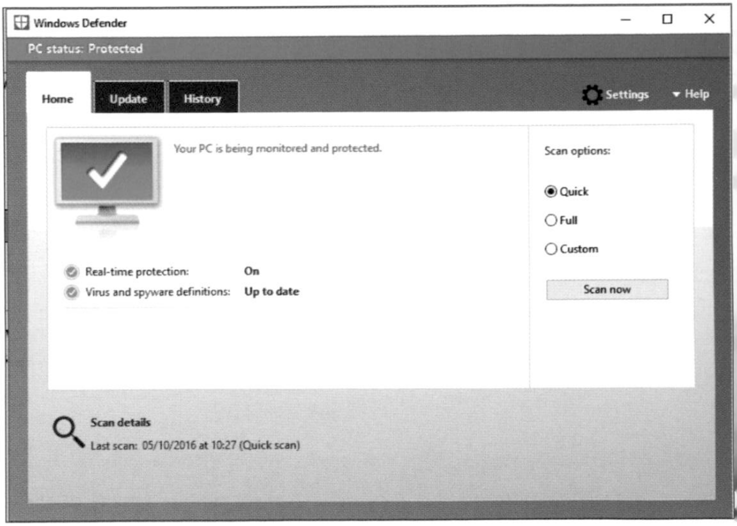

Fig. 1.14 The Windows Defender PC Status.

It is important to scan your computer occasionally to make sure that you are protected.

2

New Menus & Screens

The Windows 10 Anniversary Screens

When you restart your computer, the **Start** screen, shown in Fig. 2.1, appears on your display. Swiping upwards or pressing any key on the keyboard, displays a second screen in which you enter your user password. After that is completed, Windows displays a screen similar to that of Fig. 2.2 on the next page.

Fig. 2.1 A Windows 10 Start Screen.

> **Note:** Most swipe movements of your finger on a touch sensitive screen correspond to dragging the mouse pointer on a PC. Tapping on such a device corresponds to clicking the left mouse button, while touching and holding corresponds to a right-click of the mouse button.

The Windows Left-click Start Menu

Fig. 2.2 The Desktop with the Start Menu Activated.

The **Start** screen in the **Windows 10 Update** has changed a bit from the one in **Windows 10**. The **All apps** menu option has been removed, so now you must either scroll to find the app you want or left-click the hash (#) button below the list of **Most used** apps (also see Fig. 2.6, page 17) to open Fig. 2.3.

Fig. 2.3 A List of Letters to Use to Jump to the Required App.

If you know the name of the app you are looking for, just click the first letter of its name on the displayed screen to jump to the beginning of the group of apps that start with that letter.

Also note that the desktop background has changed. More about this shortly.

The Windows Right-click Start Menu

If you like to change the **Desktop** background picture to one of your own photos, then right-click the **Start** button (or touch and hold, then release), followed by left-clicking or tapping the **Control Panel** entry pointed to on the screen shown in Fig. 2.4.

This opens the **Control Panel** screen (part of which is shown below) in which you select the **Personalisation** option.

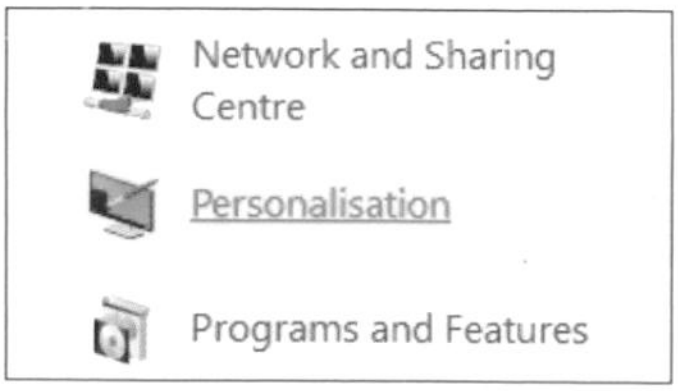

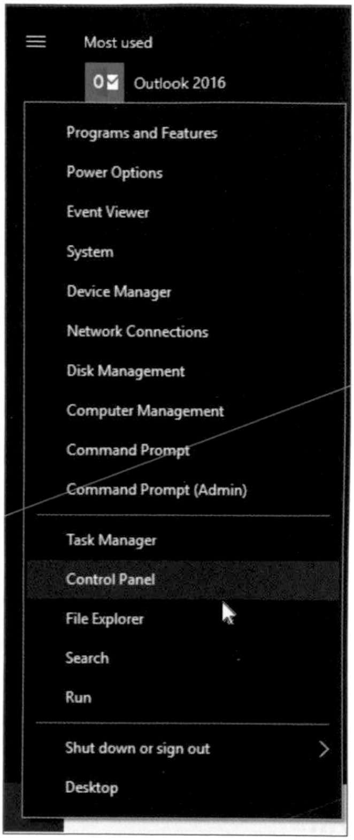

Fig. 2.4 The Right-click Start Menu.

On the displayed screen shown in Fig. 2.5 on the next page, select **Desktop Background**, then on the **Settings** screen, tap or click the **Browse** button and navigate to a folder with your best pictures.

You can also control the **Colour** and **Sounds** of the selected **Desktop Background** screen by tapping or clicking the appropriate icons shown at the bottom of the **Pesonalisation** screen, shown in the composite of Fig. 2.5 on the next page.

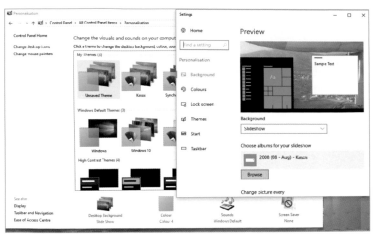

Fig. 2.5 The Composite Personalisation Screens.

Alternatively, if all this is too much for you, you could always choose not to change anything and go with the **Windows 10 Anniversary** group of photos and default sounds. I leave it to you!

Manipulating the Apps Screen

It is possible to increase the screen area that displays the various apps of a left-click **Start** menu (see Fig. 2.2, on page 14) to display more apps on the same screen without the need to scroll.

Using a Non-touch PC Screen

You can increase the number of apps on display of a PC without a touch screen by dragging the right edge of the current screen box to the right, as shown in Fig. 2.6 on the next page. In this way, you can accommodate up to three columns of grouped apps across the screen.

To return to the original screen size of one column of grouped apps, simply drag the double-arrow to the left.

Fig. 2.6 Increasing the Display Area Containing Apps.

Using a Tablet or a Touch Sensitive Screen PC

To increase the number of apps displayed on a screen of a Tablet or a touch-sensitive PC, either tap on the **Action Centre** icon pointed to at the extreme bottom right-corner of the screen in Fig. 2.7, to open the **Action Centre**. To see a full screen of apps, tap or click the **Tablet mode** icon, also pinted to in the composite screen in Fig. 2.7.

Fig. 2.7 A Composite of the Action Centre With a Full Screen of Apps.

Deselecting the **Tablet mode**, returns the screen to the usual one-column app menu.

To switch between the **Desktop** and an app screen, tap or click the **Start** button or press the **Windows**  key on the keyboard, then tap or click on the app of your choice. To return to the **Desktop** screen, close the app window by tapping or clicking on its **Close** button ✕ at the top right corner of the screen – it only lights up red when the mouse pointer is placed on it, otherwise it is grey, as are the other two buttons next to it.

Power, Settings & File Explorer Buttons

The four buttons above the **Start** button on the screen in Fig. 2.8, give you options to control **Power**, **Settings**, and the **File Explorer**. The top button tells you who is logged on at the time.

To see what each of these buttons does, do the following:

For a **PC** with a keyboard, point the mouse to each button in turn to reveal a label describing its use.

For a **Tablet**, tap the **Expand** button (the three horizontal lines at the very top of the **Start** menu screen, pointed to in Fig. 2.8, to display the screen in Fig. 2.9 shown on the next page.

Fig. 2.8 The Left-click Start Menu.

Fig. 2.9 The Expanded
Tablet Left-click Start Menu.

To revert to the normal left-click screen, tap the **Start** menu at the top of the screen in Fig. 2.9.

Tapping or clicking the button identifying the current user, displays a sub-menu, as shown here, from where you can carry out the displayed options.

Tapping or clicking the **File Explorer** button, displays the screen in Fig. 2.10 below.

Fig. 2.10 The Settings Screen.

As you can see, from the **Settings** screen you can reach screens that deal with the **System**, **Devices**, **Network & Internet** and the other listed options. I leave it to you to investigate these as they do not defer from those in the previous Windows 10 version of the Operating System.

Similarly, the **Power** button displays options for putting your computer to one of the three states: **Sleep**, **Shut down** or **Restart**.

Changing the Active Hours

To stop your computer from performing a **Restart** when you are in the middle of working so as to finish installing an update, you can change the active hours during which no **Restart** can take place. To achieve this, tap or click on **Start**, and select **Settings**, then the **Update & security** option (see Figs 2.9 and 2.10 on previous page). This opens the **Update status** dialogue box shown in Fig. 2.11 below.

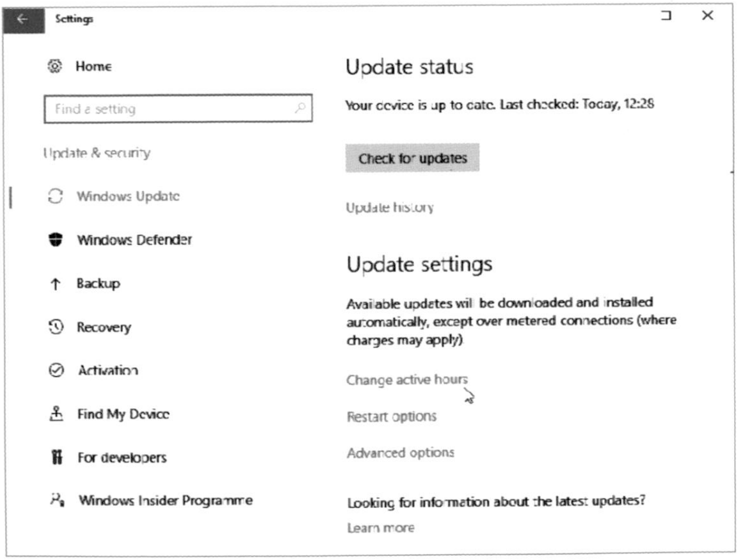

Fig. 2.11 The Update Status Dialogue Box in Settings.

Next, tap or click on **Change active hours** option, pointed to in Fig, 2.11 on the previous page, to display the screen shown in Fig. 2.12 below.

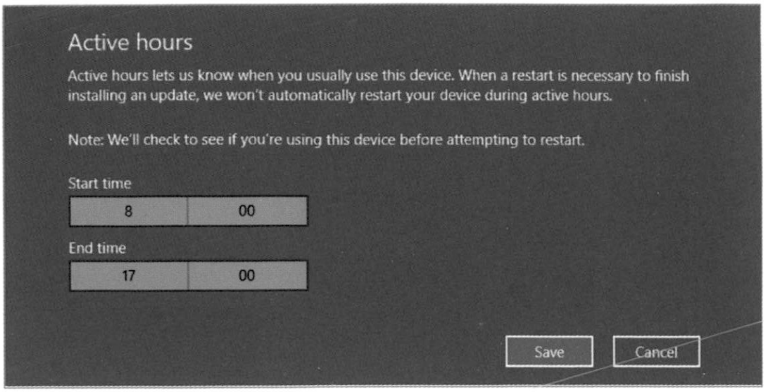

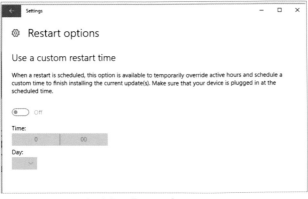

Fig. 2.12 Changing the Active Hours.

On the above screen you can set **Start time** (say 8.00) and a **End time** (say 17.00) during which time Windows is prevented from performing a **Restart**. To complete your changes, tap or click the **Save** button.

Should you require to temporarily override the chosen **Active hours**, use the **Restart options** in Fig. 2.11 on the previous page, to open the screen below.

Fig. 2.13 The Restart Options Screen.

Finally, use the **Advanced options** in Fig. 2.11 (page 20) to choose how updates are installed, as shown in Fig. 2.14 below.

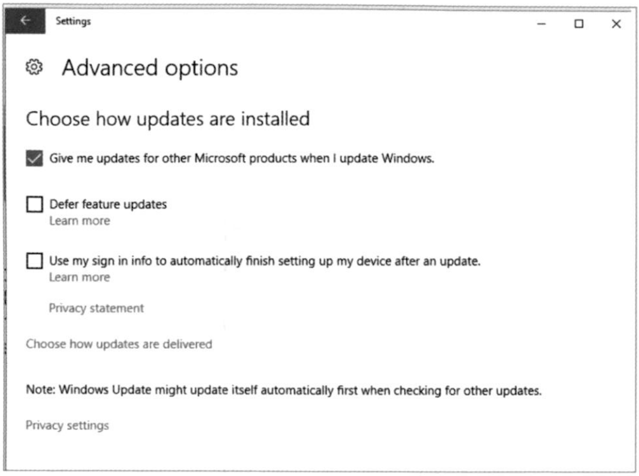

Fig. 2.14 The Advanced Options Screen.

3

OneDrive, Printers & PDFs

What is New in OneDrive

OneDrive, the cloud storage available to users, is pre-installed on **Windows 10 Anniversary Update** and can be found in the **Start** menu tiles, shown here to the right. If you used **OneDrive** before, all the documents you saved on it will still be there.

Microsoft has decreased the free storage on **OneDrive** from 30 GB (15 GB for documents and additional 15 GB for uploaded phone photos) down to 5 GB, as from 31st January 2016. You could, however, have access to 1 TB of storage if you are an Office 365 subscriber.

For some time now, I've had problems with **OneDrive**. I used **SkyDrive** (as it was known then) on my Toshiba laptop when running **Windows 7** and kept a lot of information on it. Updating directly to **Windows 10** and recently to **Windows 10 Anniversary**, retained the original content on **OneDrive** correctly.

However, on my second laptop, an Acer, not all the content of **OneDrive** was visible. Missing files had not been synced (downloaded and stored from the cloud to my laptop), which would have taken valuable space on this laptop.

The Store-based OneDrive App

Recently, Microsoft introduced the **OneDrive** app which can run on PCs, Macs, tablets and other handheld devices. This app is available on Microsoft's **Store**, and I suggest you downloaded it, as I show for my Acer laptop in Fig. 3.1 on the next page.

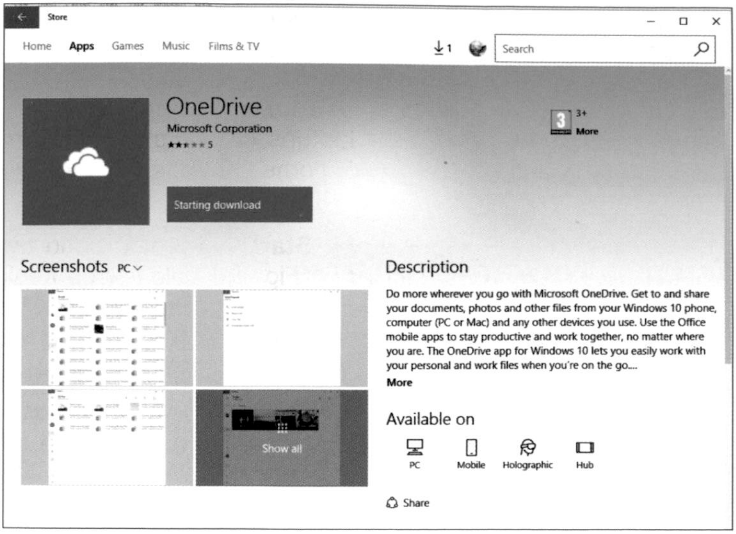

Fig. 3.1 Downloading the OneDrive App from Microsoft's Store.

After installation, you are treated to a few illustrating screens on what you can achieve by using **OneDrive**, then the final installation screen is displayed, as shown in Fig. 3.2 below.

Fig. 3.2 The Final Installation OneDrive App Screen.

On tapping or clicking the **Start Using OneDrive** button in Fig. 3.2 on the previous page, the newly installed **OneDrive** app on my Acer laptop, finds and displays all my saved work kept on **OneDrive**, originally created and kept on my Toshiba laptop. For the fist time, both laptops can display the same **OneDrive** content, even though some of these files are not stored on both laptops!

Now looking at the apps in the **Start** menu, you'll find two entries for **OneDrive**, as shown in Fig. 3.3 below. You could rename their shortcuts on the **Desktop** (drag them to the **Desktop)** to 'OneDrive Web' for the built-in one in **Windows 10**, and 'OneDrive App' for the downloaded from the **Store**.

Fig. 3.3 The Start Menu Apps List.

In my case, in Fig. 3.3, the Web-based **OneDrive** displays at the top of the **Start** menu list with the Store-based one below it.

I then downloaded the new Store-based **OneDrive** app onto my Toshiba laptop, to satisfy myself that both laptops showed the same **OneDrive** content.

Offloading Files

To offload some files (held on a computer) and keep them on **OneDrive**, then have them removed from the computer's hard drive, do the following:

Go to the extreme right of your **Taskbar** and locate the Web-based **OneDrive** icon – the one that looks like a white cloud (you might have to look in the hidden part of the **Taskbar**

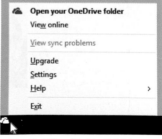

Fig. 3.4 The Right-click Menu.

icons to find it). Next, touch and hold or right-click the icon to display the context menu shown in Fig. 3.4 and select the **Settings** menu option.

This opens the **OneDrive** dialogue box shown in Fig. 3.5 with the **Account** tab selected.

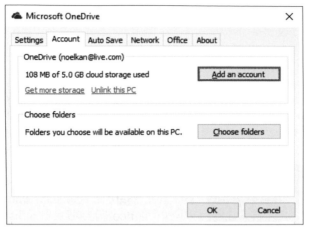

Fig. 3.5 The OneDrive Account Dialogue Box.

Tap or click the **Choose folders** to display the screen in Fig. 3.6 below.

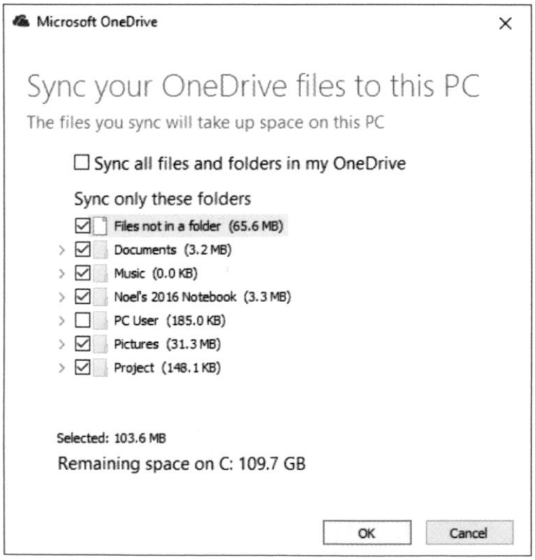

Folders with a tick, will sync with your PC, meaning that the folder will be downloaded to your PC.

Removing a tick from a folder will leave that folder on the cloud, but will remove it from your PC, giving you more space on your PC.

Fig. 3.6 The Sync OneDrive Screen.

To recover folders on the cloud and keep them on your PC, repeat the process described on the previous page, but tick the required folder, then tap or click **OK** to sync them back to your PC.

Printing Problems After the Update

In this section, I return to the error flagged during the forced download of the **Windows Anniversary Update**, namely that something was wrong with my printer. You, of course, might not encounter this problem or you might have a different one.

In fact, some users experienced much bigger problem with the update, but I can only deal with the problem I have encountered which manifest itself when I tried to print a letter, or anything else for that matter, after the update was completed. **Windows** informed me that there was no printer drivers available.

To correct this, I right-clicked the **Start** button and selected **Control Panel** from the displayed menu shown in Fig. 3.7 which opened the **Control Panel** screen, part of which is shown in Fig. 3.8 on the next page.

Programs and Features

Mobility Center

Power Options

Event Viewer

System

Device Manager

Network Connections

Disk Management

Computer Management

Command Prompt

Command Prompt (Admin)

Task Manager

Control Panel

File Explorer

Search

Run

Shut down or sign out   >

Desktop

Ask me anything

Fig. 3.7 The Right-click Start Menu.

On the displayed **All Control Panel Items** screen, part of which is shown in Fig. 3.8 below, I selected the **Devices and Printers** option, pointed to on the screen below, which opened the **Devices and Printers** screen.

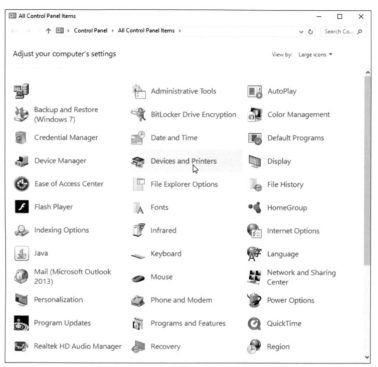

Fig. 3.8 Part of the Control Panel Screen.

Originally, the displayed **Devices and Printers** screen had no devices or printers showing, but when I tapped the **Add a printer** option it populated the screen with all my devices and printers, together with a number of other printers, as shown in Fig. 3.9 on the next page.

Amongst the various installed printers a new **Microsoft Print to PDF** printer appeared which, in principle, should make the creation of PDF (Portable Document Format) files a lot easier, if you did not use **Microsoft Word** or have such expensive programs as **Adobe Acrobat**.

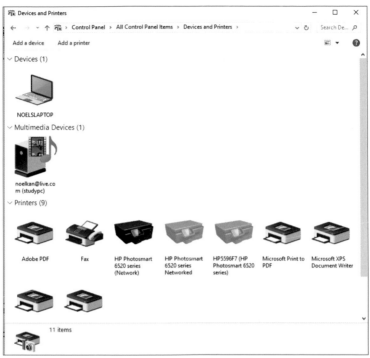

Fig. 3.9 The Devices and Printers Screen.

The inclusion of the **Microsoft Print to PDF**, is a welcome alternative to expensive programs such as **Adobe Acrobat**, or so I thought at the time!

Creating PDF Files

Many large documents that you encounter on the Internet, ebooks, etc., including this book, are produced in PDF file format with a **.pdf** file extension and represented by the icon shown here. PDF is a file that preserves the fonts, graphic images and layout of the original source document, regardless of the application used to create or view it. Such files are compact and can be shared, viewed and printed by anyone using the freely available **Adobe Reader**.

To create a PDF file, simply print your document (in this case
the chapter I am writing now) to a PDF printer (in this instant
to the **Microsoft Print to PDF** printer, as shown in Fig. 3.10.

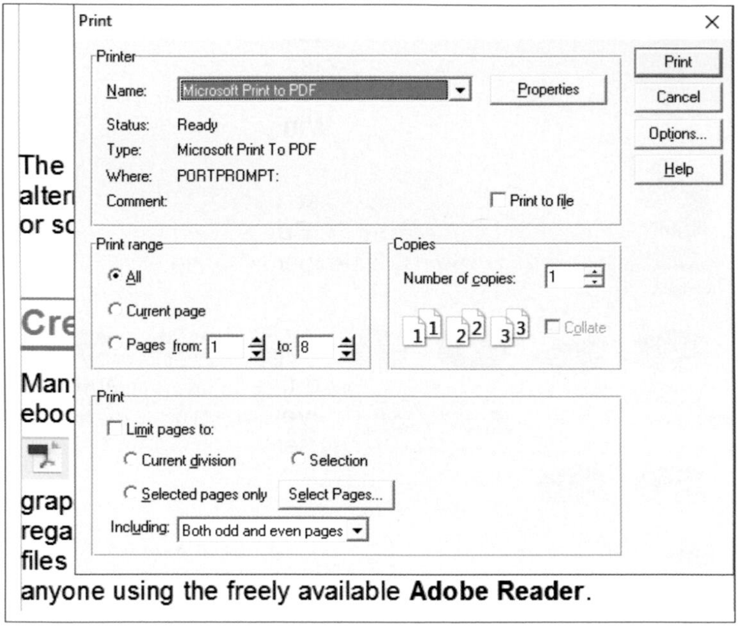

anyone using the freely available **Adobe Reader**.

Fig. 3.10 Printing to a PDF Printer.

That was extremely easy and straight forward – all I had to do
was verify that the resultant PDF complied with all the
necessary specifications for the publication of the book, such
as the inclusion of all the fonts and the inclusion of the correct
subtractive colour model specification CMYK (**C**yan, **M**agenta,
Yellow and blac**K**).

Although all the fonts were present in the resultant PDF,
the colour of the images were in RGB (**R**ed, **G**reen and **B**lue)
which is an additive colour model, not suitable for accurate
representation of coloured images.

Pity that Microsoft did not see fit to use their excellent PDF
creation program built into Microsoft **Word** which complies
with all the requirements for publishing work. Perhaps they
will in the future!

Note: Since starting to write this book, there have been three updates of **Windows 10 Anniversary**. In fact, prior to the latest update, my **Adobe Acrobat 7 Pro** program did not work. Every time I tried to use it, I was told that it wasn't compatible with **Windows 10 Anniversary**.

However, since the last update (29th October 2016), it worked. But, a day later and after a **Restart**, it stopped working!

I do hope that by the time you read this book, this and other shortcomings in **Windows 10 Anniversary** would have been iron out to the satisfaction of all its users!

4

What is New in Cortana

Cortana has taken a face lift in the **Anniversary Update**, so now it can keep up with the competition from rivals, such as **Siri** on Apple devices, **Google Assistant** on Google's latest **Pixel** phone and **Alexa** on Amazon.

Cortana can now be accessed on the **Lock Screen**, that is on the screen before you sign in with your **Password**.

> **Note:** Access to **Cortana** on the **Lock Screen** can only be achieved after you configure **Cortana** to respond to the voice command "**Hey Cortana**".

Lock Screen Access to Cortana

Next to the **Start** button, is **Cortana**, at the very bottom of your screen, as shown in Fig. 4.1.

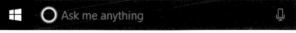

Fig. 4.1 Cortana, the Digital Assistant.

In **Windows 10**, **Cortana** only displays after you sign in using your **Password**.

However, in **Windows 10 Anniversary Update** you can configure **Cortana** so it can be accessed on the **Lock Screen**. To do so, tap or click on it, where it displays the words "**Ask me anything**", to open **Cortana**'s **Home** screen shown in Fig. 4.2 on the next page, with its **Home** button shown highlighted.

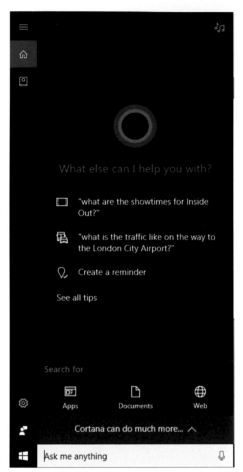

Fig. 4.2 Cortana's Home Screen With Some Suggestions.

Cortana's Settings

Tapping or clicking **Cortana**'s **Settings** button at the bottom-left of the screen in Fig. 4.2, also shown here, displays the screen in Fig. 4.3 on the next page, where you can configure **Cortana** so it can be accessed from the **Lock Screen**.

Fig. 4.3 Cortana's Settings Screen.

Under **Hey Cortana,** turn the option to **On** (its default setting is **Off**, as shown above). The moment you turn this option to **On**, more options appear below it, as shown here in Fig. 4.4.

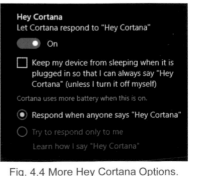

Don't forget to check the **Let Cortana access my calendar, email**, etc., box in Fig. 4.3 before going on.

Fig. 4.4 More Hey Cortana Options.

There are a lot more options on the **Settings** screen, but to see them all, you'll have to either swipe upwards or scroll down. It is worth spending sometime here, examining all the options offered. Make sure the language is set to English UK.

Next, put your computer to sleep, either by closing the lid (if you have configured it to do so), or by tapping or clicking the **Power** button (see Fig. 2.8, page 18), then wake up your computer and on the **Lock Screen** (and before signing in) say the words "**Hey Cortana**, what films are showing near me?"

In this case, **Cortana** responds with a voice message (rather too quick to understand) and the screen shown in Fig. 4.5.

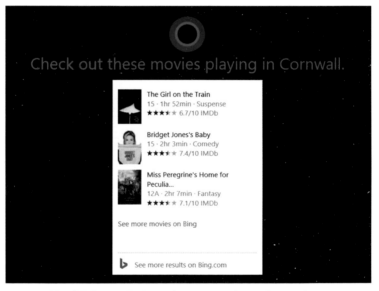

Fig. 4.5 Cortana's Home Screen With Some Suggestions.

So far, **Cortana** worked well – not so, though, with my next specific test, namely sending an e-mail to a contact with a name that **Cortana** doesn't quite comprehend, because the spelling of the said name is not in **Cortana**'s way of thinking!

Using Cortna to Send an E-mail

Having woken up **Cortana**, by either saying "**Hey Cortana**" or by tapping or clicking the microphone shown at the bottom-right corner in Fig. 4.2 (page 34), then I said "new e-mail please to Rachael Kantaris". In Fig. 4.6, I display **Cortana**'s answer.

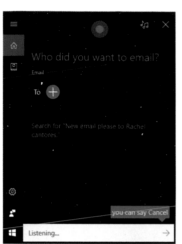

Fig. 4.6 Using Cortana to Send a New E-mail.

Sadly, **Cortana** only seems to use the 'modern' spelling for names (Rachel instead of Rachael), so it can't find the recipient, even if it got the surname correct, which mostly it did not!

No matter how many times I repeated the recipient's name, **Cortana** could not find the e-mail address associated with that name and eventually asked me to help her by typing it in, which I did, as shown in Fig. 4.7.

After that, I had to tap or click the microphone to wake up **Cortana** again and anything I said from there on, was taken to be the actual e-mail message.

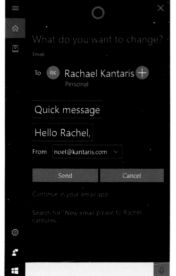

Fig. 4.7 Dictating a Message.

Any hesitation, no matter how short, was taken by **Cortana** to be the end of the message and I was asked immediately whether the message should be sent.

Although I could select to add or change my message or

Fig. 4.8 A Successful E-mail.

the subject of the e-mail (which I had not been asked to provide in the first place), by the time I got everything right, it would had been a lot easier and quicker to just use my regular e-mail program!

Having said that, getting **Cortana** to send an e-mail to a less problematic name, is very easy. For example, saying **Hey Cortana**, send an e-mail to **Adrian**, then dictating the message, produced the result shown in Fig. 4.8 (the recipient's surname has been obscured, so as to preserve anonymity).

Getting Directions

To find out how far a place is from your location and get directions, simply say **Hey Cortana, how far to Redruth**. I chose the town of 'Redruth' as it is near where I live, though you should choose a place near you instead, so you can see clearly the result and check the directions given!

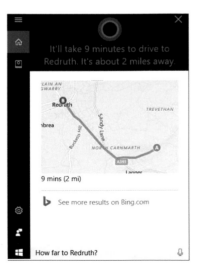

Fig. 4.9 Getting information.

Cortana's Notebook

Below **Cortana**'s **Home** button, you will find the **Notebook**
 button, also shown here on the left. To see the
captions for **Cortana**'s buttons, tap or click
the **Expand** button, shown here on the right,
so you can find out what they do.

Tapping or clicking the **Notebook** button, displays a rather
long screen, part of which is shown in Fig. 4.10 below. To see
the rest, swipe upwards or scroll downwards.

The options on the
Notebook screen lets
you do the following:

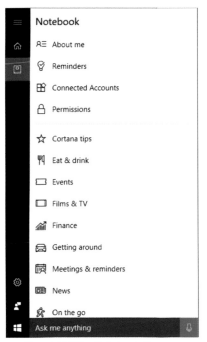

- **About me** – lets
  you change the
  information you
  hold about
  yourself. You can
  change your
  name, your
  favourite places
  and your e-mail
  address.

- **Reminders** – set
  reminders, so
  Cortana knows
  when to remind
  you to take a
  certain action,
  such as when to
  save your work,
  when to make a
  telephone call,
  when to set off for a meeting, etc.

Fig. 4.10 The Notebook Screen.

- **Connected Accounts** – connect accounts that you
  participate in, such as LinkedIn. Office 365 or Xbox
  Live, etc., so that **Cortana** can manage them more
  efficiently.

- **Permissions** – Give **Cortana** permission to track your location, to allow access to your contacts, e-mail and calendar and allow access to your browsing history.

- **Academic** – Keeps track of academic cards, conference updates News updates and New papers.

- **Cortana tips** – Provides tips from **Cortana** on suggestions, tip cards and tip notifications.

- **Eat & drink** – Allows you to set your preferences on the subject and select appropriate options.

- **Events** – Gives suggestions on local events.

- **Finance** – Allows you to track stocks you own.

- **Getting around** – Provides you with traffic notification and keeps track of your appointments.

- **Health & fitness** – Helps you to reach your goals.

- **Meetings & reminders** – Helps you to know what comes next in your diary.

- **Movies** & TV – Allows you to see times of shows and trailers.

- **News** – Allows **Cortana** to inform you on news stories that interest you.

- **On the go** – While out and about, **Cortana** can offer to help you with tasks that interest you.

- **Packages** – Keeps track of your have sent or ones that are on their way to you.

Clearly you must examine these many options in **Cortana** carefully, because some default ones must be turned off, while others must be turned on, otherwise **Cortana** will not be able to meet your requirements or might run your life for you!

One setting you might like to look at, especially if you have youngsters in your family, is the **Bing SafeSearch Settings** to be found at the very bottom of the **Settings** screen, as shown in Fig. 4.11 on the next page. This allows you to inhibit **Bing** from displaying adult content on searches.

Some **Settings** are only relevant to your location and to whether you have configured **Cortana** on a mobile device that you carry around with you.

For example, you can ask **Cortana**, to remind you to phone a friend when you get to work. It certainly works, but I leave that to you to experiment with, if you have an Android or a Windows operated smart phone!

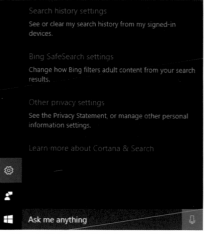

Fig. 4.11 Bing's SafeSearch Setting.

Cortana's Reminding Capabilities

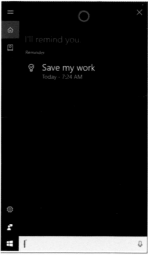

Fig. 4.12 A Cortana Promise.

Many users, including myself, have experienced problems with reminders and **Cortana's Notifications**. For example, you ask **Cortana** to remind you to, say, 'save my work in 5 min' and although **Cortana** responds with **I'll remind you**, as shown in Fig. 4.12, time passes, and nothing happens!

This is because the **Notifications** settings are set to **Off** by default! To remedy this, use the **Start** menu, then tap or click the **Settings** button to display the screen shown in Fig. 4.13 on the next page.

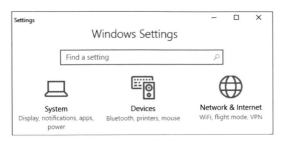

Fig. 4.13 Part of the Settings Screen.

In Fig. 4.13, select **System**, then **Notifications & actions** and on the displayed screen shown in Fig. 4.14 below, turn the option **Get notifications from apps and other senders** to **On**.

Settings	— □ ×

⚙ Home

| Find a setting | 🔍 |

System

🖵 Display

🗏 Apps & features

🗐 Default apps

🔲 Notifications & actions

⏻ Power & sleep

🖴 Battery

🖴 Storage

🗺 Offline maps

🖵 Tablet mode

🖵 Multitasking

🖵 Projecting to this PC

🖵 Apps for websites

ⓘ About

Quick actions

Press and hold (or select) quick actions, then drag to rearrange them. These quick actions appear in action center.

Tablet mode	Network	Note	All settings
Airplane mode	Location	Quiet hours	Brightness
Bluetooth	VPN	Battery saver	Project
Connect			

Add or remove quick actions

Notifications

Get notifications from apps and other senders

⬤ Off

Show notifications on the lock screen
⬤ On

Show alarms, reminders, and incoming VoIP calls on the lock screen
⬤ On

Hide notifications when I'm duplicating my screen
⬤ Off

Fig. 4.14 The Settings Screen.

Now, asking **Cortana** to remind you to save your work, produces the display shown in Fig. 4.15, after the specified time interval.

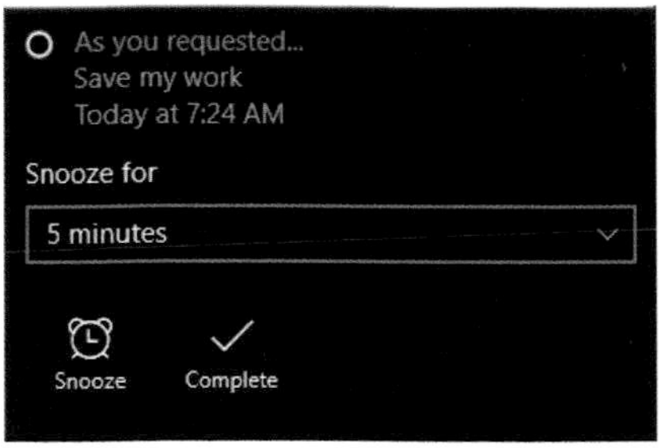

Fig. 4.15 Cortana's Reminder.

This reminder will remain on the   bottom right-hand side of your **Desktop** screen, until you tap or click **Complete** or the **Snooze** period expires.

The above remedy works well with one of my laptops, but the other one displays the **Get notifications from apps and other senders** switch (Fig. 4.14 on the previous page), greyed out which means you cannot switch it to **On**. With some computers this can be fixed by changing the **Registry**, in particular by modifying the

NoToastApplicationNotifications to '**0**'.

To do this, use **Regedit** then go to:

HKEY_CURRENT_USERS\Software\Policies\Microsoft\ Windows\CurrentVersion\PusNotifications

then right-click on **NoToastApplicationNotifications**, select **Modify** in the pop-up box and enter '**0**' in the **Value data** field. This worked for me!

If the above instructions sounds gibberish to you, get an expert to do the job!

Note: Changing the **Registry** is extremely dangerous if you don't know what you are doing – you could make your computer inoperable. Even experts are advised to make a backup of the **Registry** before changing anything. **Be warned!**

One explanation for the differences between my two laptops could be attributed to the fact that one laptop was upgraded directly from Windows 7 to Windows 10, while the other one (the troublesome with respect to notifications) was upgraded via Windows 8, then 8.1 before going to Windows 10.

Many expert users are of the opinion that upgrading via Windows 8 and 8.1, to Windows 10, retains a lot of unwanted baggage from these previous versions!

Cortana, E-mail & Calendar

When you receive an e-mail with a suggested meeting, giving date and times, **Cortana** is supposed to automatically insert this appointment into your **Calendar**. That, of course presupposes that you are using as your mailing program either **Mail**, the new **Outlook** or a **Live** account.

To test this supposition, I prepared the e-mail shown in Fig. 4.16 using my **Microsoft Office Outlook** program and sent it to myself to my new **Outlook live.com** account.

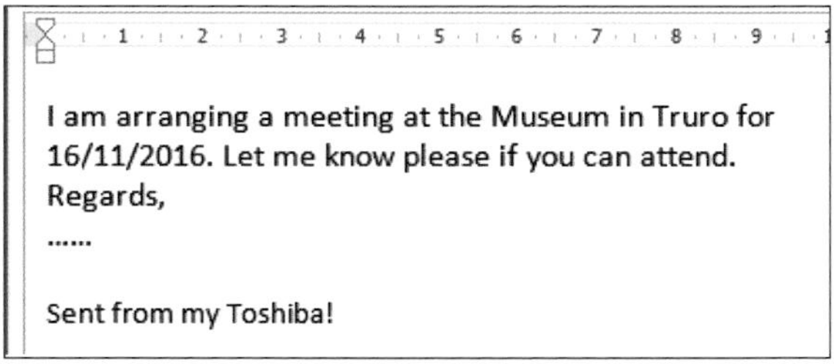

Fig. 4.16 E-mail sent to my Live Account.

Rather confusingly, Microsoft named their new, rather simple **Outlook** e-mail program by the same name as their superior **Office Outlook** e-mail and P/A program!

I sent the same e-mail shown above several times to my **live.com** account, but each time, I varied the way I wrote the date, to see to which date format **Cortana** best reacted to. I used three different date formats; 16th November, 2016, 16/11/2016 and Wednesday 16th of November.

One can check that **Mail** has been configured correctly by going to **Settings**, **Manage Accounts**, as shown in Fig. 4.17.

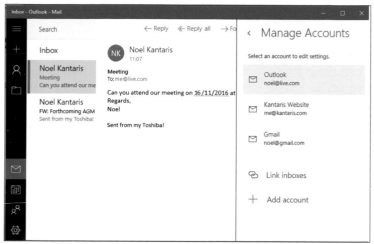

Fig. 4.17 The Manage Accounts Settings in Mail.

After receiving each of the first two e-mail messages, I opened the **Calendar** in **Mail**, as shown in Fig. 4.18.

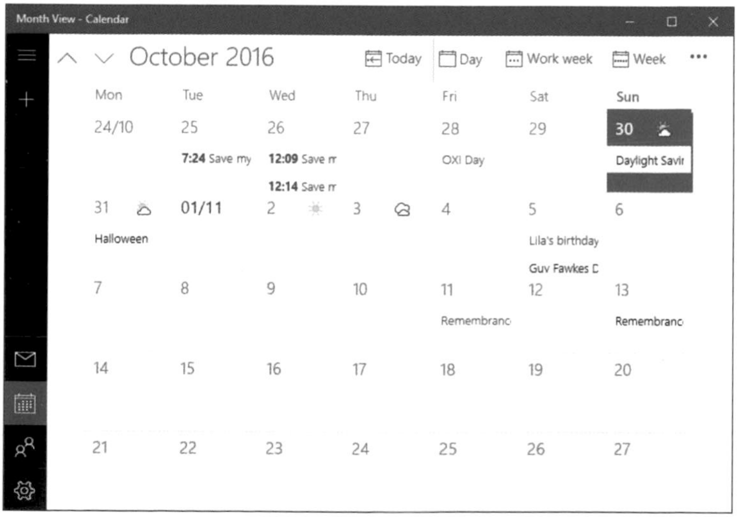

Fig. 4.18 The Calendar in Mail.

It is interesting that there is no entry in **Calendar** about a meeting on 16th November (see Fig. 4.18 on previous page), but my attempts to have **Cortana** remind me to save my work, are recorded instead!

The last e-mail with the date format Wednesday 16th of November, when received, it had the date underlined with small dots. Placing the mouse pointer on this date, it turned the mouse pointer into a pointing hand. Clicking on this date, displayed the screen below.

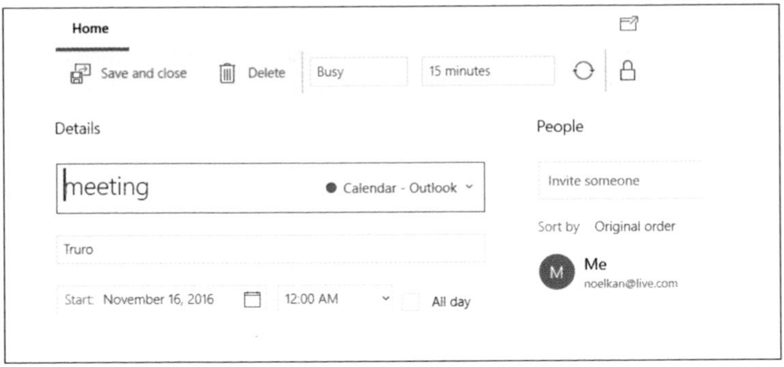

Fig. 4.19 The Calendar in Mail Detecting a Meeting.

This time, the **Calendar** opened on the correct date with the correct venue and waited for me to insert the time and duration of the meeting.

Hopefully Microsoft will sort out these discrepancies very soon.

5

The Taskbar & Action Centre

The Taskbar Area

Next to the **Start** button, is **Cortana** and to the right of that is
the **Taskbar**. The icons (also referred to as buttons) of the
apps on the **Taskbar**, shown in Fig. 5.1, are the **Task View**,
the **Microsoft Edge** browser, the **File Explorer** and the
Windows **Store**.

Fig. 5.1 Part of the Taskbar.

Other icons or buttons to the right of these, can activate
programs that you have installed and pinned to the **Taskbar**.
For my PC, such program icons are shown separately in
Fig. 5.2

Fig. 5.2 Icons of Installed Programs Pinned on the Taskbar.

A faint blue line under a program icon, indicates that the
program is running. The last icon in Fig. 5.2 is that of the
Internet Explorer. However, with **Windows 10 Anniversary**,
Microsoft now prefers us to use the **Edge** browser as it is
capable now of supporting third party plug-ins.

The Right-click Taskbar Menu

Placing the mouse pointer in between the **Task View** and
Microsoft Edge browser icons and right-clicking, displays the
menu shown in Fig. 5.3 on the next page. The same menu
appears if you touch and hold at the same point on the
screen.

You must be careful, though, not to activate the app on either side of the point you have chosen to click.

Address	Toolbars	>
Links	Cortana	>
Desktop	✓ Show Task View button	
New toolbar...	Show Windows Ink Workspace button	
	✓ Show touch keyboard button	
	Cascade windows	
	Show windows stacked	
	Show windows side by side	
	Show the desktop	
	Task Manager	
	Lock the taskbar	
	✿ Settings	

Fig. 5.3 The Right-click Taskbar Menu Also Displaying the
Toolbars Sub-menu.

The Toolbars Sub-menu

The right-click menu is new to this version of **Windows 10**. You can use the **Toolbars** sub-menu to activate the **Desktop** option by selecting it which introduces the **Shink/Expand** icon on the extreme right of the **Taskbar** as well as the **Desktop** icon next to it, as shown in Fig. 5.4 below.

Fig. 5.4 The Shrink/Expand
and Desktop Icons.

Clicking the down-arrowhead on the **Shink/Expand** icon, removes the icons on the **Taskbar** (except for the last one), while clicking the up-arrowhead reinstates them.

Clicking the pair of arrowheads on the **Desktop** icon, displays all the shortcuts on your desktop, part of which are shown in Fig. 5.5 for my laptop.

Clicking again the pair of arrowheads on the **Desktop** icon, hides the desktop shortcuts.

To return to the normal **Taskbar** screen, right-click an empty part of the **Taskbar** and remove the check mark against the **Desktop** sub-menu of the **Toolbars** menu (see Fig. 5.3 on the previous page).

The Cortana Sub-menu

Fig. 5.5 Part of the Desktop shortcuts for my Laptop.

Next, select **Cortana** on the right-click **Taskbar** menu to open the sub-menu shown here in Fig. 5.6.

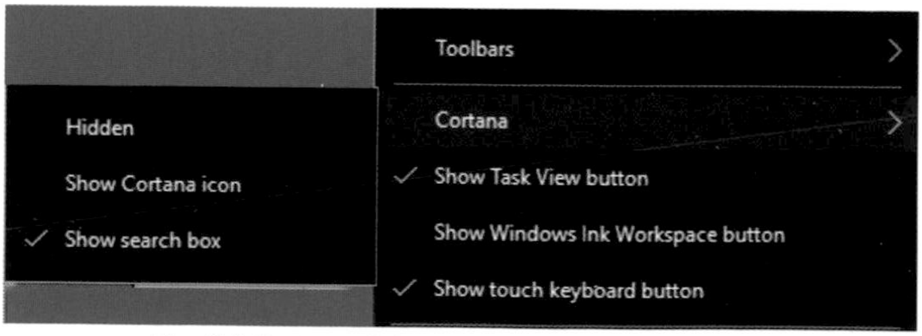

Fig. 5.6 Cortana Sub-menu of the Taskbar Menu

From here you can choose to hide **Cortana** altogether, or simply reduce it to an icon. I prefer to have **Cortana** showing with a search box, so no changes here!

As you can see in Fig. 5.3 shown on the previous page, there are a lot more options you can choose to suit the way you work, so I leave it to you to experiment and find out what you prefer.

The Taskbar Settings Menu

Selecting the **Settings** option of the **Taskbar** menu (see Fig. 5.3, page 48), displays the screen shown in Fig. 5.7.

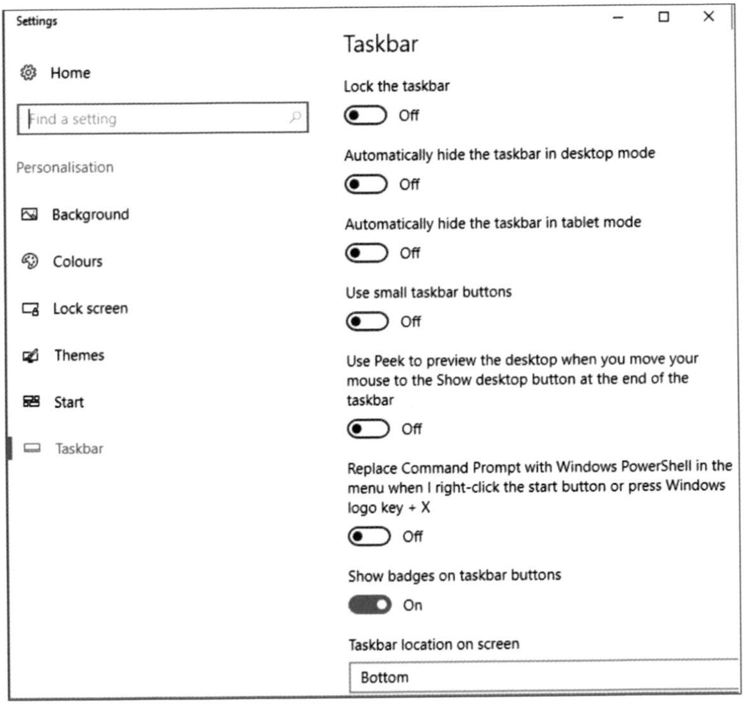

Fig. 5.7 The Settings Screen for the Taskbar.

From here, you can choose to **Lock the Taskbar**, **Automatically hide the taskbar in desktop mode**, **Use small taskbar buttons**, etc. There is a lot of choices to be made, especially as only part of the **Taskbar Settings** screen is shown above. You'll have to either swipe upwards or scroll downwards to see the rest of the available options.

While on the **Settings** screen, you might like to examine other options, such as **Personisation**, **Background**, **Colours**, etc. Do spend some time looking at these. As you select each of these options, different **Settings** screens are displayed.

The Action Centre

To the right of the **Taskbar** you'll find new icons in the **Action Centre**, also known as the **System Tray**. Icons shown here in Fig. 5.8, are: **Show hidden icons**, **Battery charge** status, **Internet access** indicator, the **Touch keyboard**, the **Time and Date** indicator and the **Notifications** button.

Fig. 5.8 The Action Centre, Also Known as the System Tray.

If you tap or click the up-arrowhead icon (first on the left), the **Hidden icons** in the **System Tray** are displayed, as shown in Fig. 5.9 for my laptop.

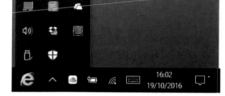

Fig. 5.9 The Hidden Icons in the System Tray.

Placing the mouse pointer on any of these icons, automatically displays a label which tells you of its function.

Two icons on the **Action Centre** are worth looking at in more detail, as they are new to the **Windows 10 Anniversary Update**. These are the combined **Date & Time** and the **Notifications** buttons.

The Date & Time Screen

Tapping or clicking the area where the **Time & Date** are displayed on the **Action Centre**, displays the combined screen shown in Fig. 5.10 on the next page.

At the bottom of the screen in Fig. 5.10, you see 'Today's Events', if any. To hide such events, scroll down to the bottom of the screen to see the **Hide Agenda** button shown here. Tapping or clicking it, removes today's events and replaces the button on the screen to **Show Agenda**.

At the very top of the screen the time and date are displayed and in this case two more times are shown, one for California and another for Sydney where I have family. These were carried forward when I installed the Windows update.

To make any changes to the **Time & Date** screen, touch and hold or right-click that area of the **Action Centre** screen to display the what is shown in Fig. 5.11.

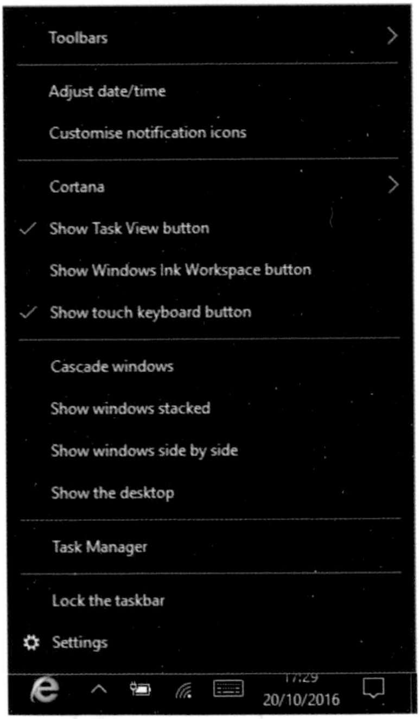

Fig. 5.10 The Combined Time and Date Screen.

This is yet another 'customisation' screen with some familiar options, as we have seen earlier.

Tapping or clicking the second option from the top, displays the **Date & Time** screen, shown in Fig. 5.12 on the next page, which allows you to make appropriate adjustments.

Fig. 5.11 The Time & Date Right-click Menu.

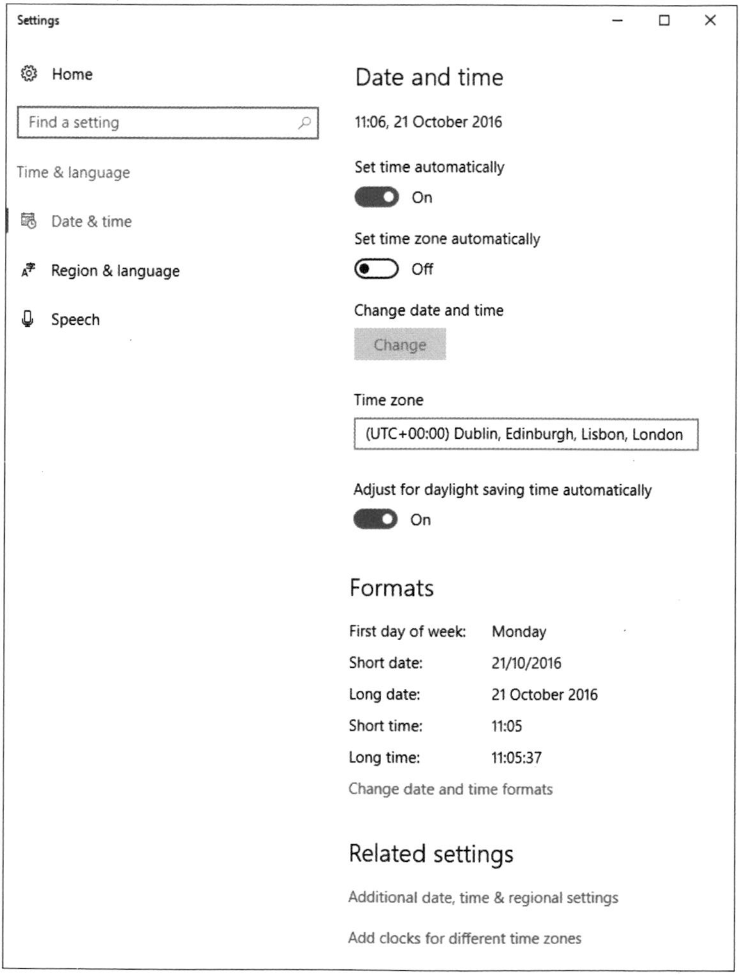

Fig. 5.12 The Settings Screen for Date & Time.

What is shown in Fig. 5.12, is a composite of the full **Date & Time** screen. For you to see the bottom part of the screen, you'll have to either swipe upwards or scroll downwards. What I wanted to show you here, is the link at the very bottom of the screen which allows you to add clocks for different time zones – essential if you are to avoid waking up friends, on the other side of the world, in the middle of the night!

Having added different time zone clocks to your system, to see what those times are at any time, just place the mouse pointer on the **Time & Date** area, to display the local and additional times, as shown here to the right.

The Notifications Screen

To the right of the **Time & Date** screen area is the new **Notifications** button. Tapping or clicking this button, displays the **Action Centre** screen, as shown in Fig. 5.13.

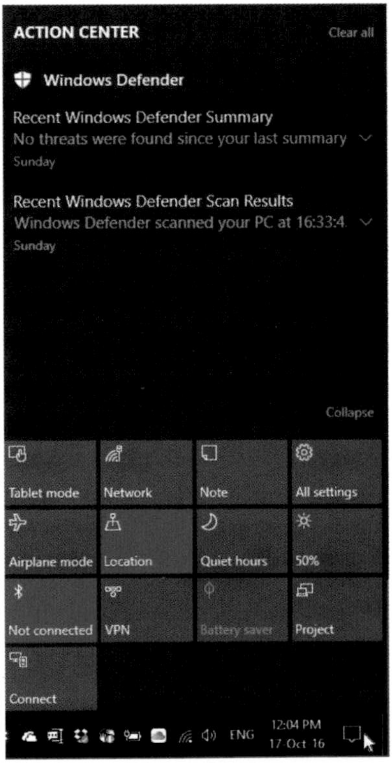

The **Action Centre** has two parts. At the top, any **Notifications** that might exist are displayed. Here, it shows that I scanned my PC last Sunday at 16.33 and no threats were found, for which I am very happy!

Any other type of **Notifications** will show at the top half of the screen. Detailed information about any such event can be seen by tapping or clicking the down-arrowhead to the right of each such event.

You can remove all **Notifications** by tapping or clicking the **Clear all** button, or you can temporarily remove the displayed events by tapping or clicking the **Collapse** button.

Fig. 5.13 The Action Centre.

The lower part of the **Action Centre**, displays various tiles you can tap or click to give you access to:

- **Tablet mode** – Turns **Tablet mode** on. When **On** it displays in blue, as do all the other options.

- **Networks** – Displays all **Networks** in your vicinity, so you can choose the right one.

- **OneNote** – Displays the **OneNote** screen, so you can make a note or two.

- **All settings** – Displays the familiar **Windows Settings** screen.

- **Flight mode** – Turns on the **Flight mode** required when in an aircraft while watching a film on your PC.

- **Location** – Turns on **Location** (in Fig. 5.13 on the previous page it displays in blue, indicating it is already on). Tapping or clicking this tile, will turn it off.

- **Quiet hours** – Turns on **Quiet hours**, necessary if your PC is next to you when asleep.

- **Brightness** – Changes the screen **Brightness**. Each time you tap or click this tile, it changes the brightness of the screen by 25%.

- **Bluetooth** – Turns on **Bluetooth** so you can communicate with similarly empowered devices.

- **VPN** – Display the **VPN** (Virtual Private Network) settings screen. A **VPN** is designed to provide encrypted connection between a remote user and a company network.

- **Battery saver** – Turns on the **Battery saver** option for when your computer is not plugged into the mains.

- **Project** – Displays the **Project** screen in which you can select to show a project on your PC's screen only, duplicate your PC's screen, extend your PC's screen or show it on a second screen only.

- **Connect** – Displays the **Connect** screen to allow you to search for wireless display and audio devices. For this to succeed, both your device and **Bluetooth** must be turned on.

6

The Microsoft Edge Browser

The Edge Browser's Opening Screen

The version of **Microsoft Edge**, the successor to **Internet Explorer**, included in **Windows 10 Anniversary Update**, now supports browser extensions. However, there are not many extensions available yet.

Installing extensions is rather simple, but first let us have a look at the program itself. To open **Microsoft Edge**, tap or click on the **Start** menu tile, also shown here. This displays the screen in Fig. 6.1 below.

Fig. 6.1 A Microsoft Edge Browser Screen.

Your opening screen might look different – I have configured **Microsoft Edge** to open with a **Google** screen rather than the endless news clips. To do this, tap or click the **Menu** button at the top-right of the screen, also shown here.

This opens the screen shown in Fig. 6.2. I shall be referring to this screen shortly when I discuss **Extensions**, but for now tap or click on **Settings** to display the screen in Fig. 6.3 on the next page.

New window	
New InPrivate window	
Zoom	— 100% +
Cast media to device	
Find on page	
Print	
Pin this page to Start	
F12 Developer Tools	
Open with Internet Explorer	
Send feedback	
Extensions	
What's new and tips	
Settings	

Fig. 6.2 The Menu Screen.

On the **Settings** screen (Fig. 6.3) and under **Open Microsoft Edge with**, tap or click the down-arrowhead and from the displayed menu choose **A specific page or pages**, then in the box below that, type:

http://google.co.uk/

then tap or click the **Save** button to the right of the **URL** button, also shown here. From now on, the opening screen when you start **Microsoft Edge**, will be **Google**.

You, of course, could choose a different search engine, a blank page, any image or the default **Start page**. The choice is yours!

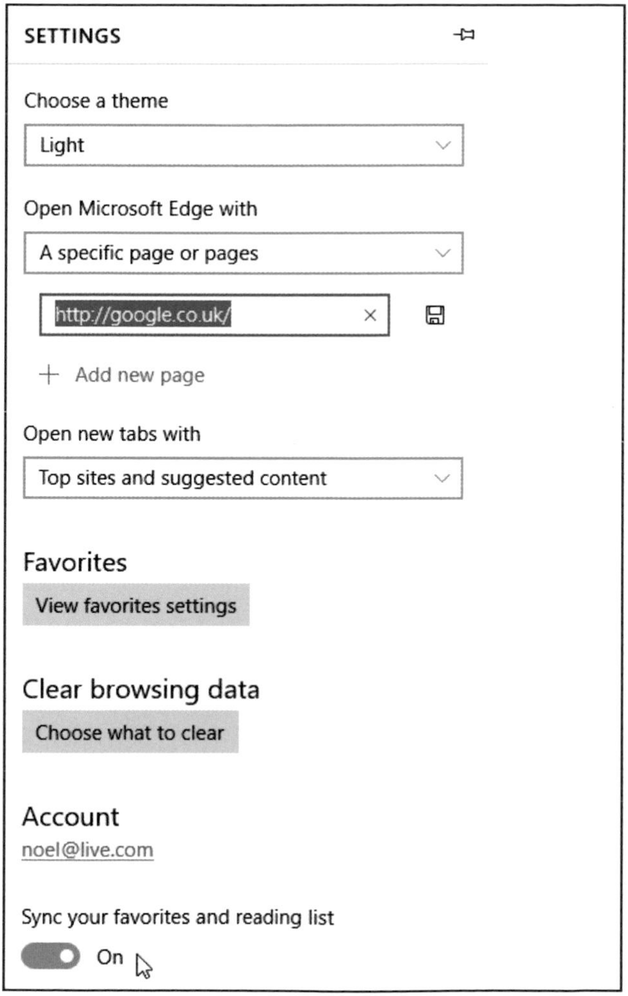

SETTINGS

Choose a theme

| Light | ∨ |

Open Microsoft Edge with

| A specific page or pages | ∨ |

| http://google.co.uk/ | × | 💾

+ Add new page

Open new tabs with

| Top sites and suggested content | ∨ |

Favorites

View favorites settings

Clear browsing data

Choose what to clear

Account
noel@live.com

Sync your favorites and reading list
On ⬤○

Fig. 6.3 Changing the Opening Screen of the Edge Browser.

Finally, turn the switch **Sync your favorites and reading list**, pointed to in Fig. 6.3, to **On.**

As a result of these changes, the opening page of **Edge** will now be clean, without the news clips, adverts and all the clatter that **Microsoft** thinks that we should be subjected to!

The Edge Browser's Extensions

As mentioned earlier, **Microsoft Edge** now supports extensions, but there are not many available at present. At the time of writing, there were 16 free extensions, as compared to the tens of thousands available for Google Chrome.

To see these extensions, tap or click the **Extensions** entry in Fig. 6.2, page 58, to display the screen shown in Fig. 6.4. The link on that screen gets you to Microsoft's **Store** where all the available extensions are shown. These are listed below.

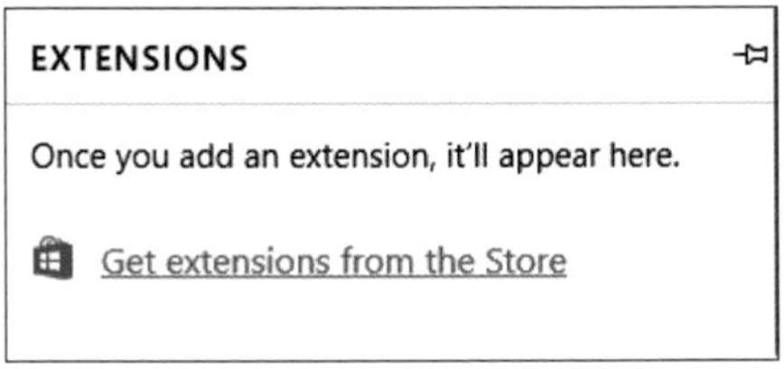

EXTENSIONS

Once you add an extension, it'll appear here.

Get extensions from the Store

Fig. 6.4 The Extension Link to Microsoft's Store Screen.

Pinterest – After getting, installing, launching it, then turning it on, the button allows you to read and change content on Websites you visit, save for later something interesting you found, such as articles, recipes, etc. However, for this to work, you must 'sign up' and select five types of interest, such as 'Art', 'Travel', 'Design', etc., so that appropriate content can be suggested to you.

Evernote Web Clipper – Use this extension to save things you see on the Web into your Evernote account. This extension creates visual clips rather than text bookmarks, but you have to 'sign up' and create an account.

Amazon Assistant – It helps you make better decisions wherever you shop online by giving you access to deals of the day and allowing product comparison. If you don't have an Amazon account already, you'll be asked to create one.

AdBlock – It helps to block ads on Websites. However there are equal number of people who love it to those that can't make it work, based on ratings and reviews!

 Adblock Plus – This extension is still in early stages of development and has known issues and limitations, according to its developers. Nevertheless, it also claims to be the most popular ad blocker on the market!

 Translator for Microsoft Edge – It can translate foreign Web pages and text selections for 50+ languages.

 LastPass: Free Password Manager – It saves your passwords and gives you secure access from every computer and mobile device.

 OneNote Web Clipper – It allows you to quickly capture Web pages to OneNote, where you can edit, annotate, or share the information.

 Office Online – It places an icon on the Microsoft Edge toolbar that gives direct access to your Office files, whether these are stored on OneDrive or on your PC.

 Save to Pocket – It allows you to save articles and videos you want to read and watch later to Pocket. You can then view them on your PC, tablet or phone.

 Reddit Enhancement Suite – This is a suite of enhancements for browsing Reddit experience. It allows you to read and change your cookies, see the Websites you visit, store personal browsing data on your device and read content on some Website and also change it.

Mouse Gestures – Allows you to perform basic browsing tasks by right-clicking and then move the mouse down and to the right to close the current tab, or move the mouse right to left to go back to the previous page. This extension doesn't work on mouse pads!

 Tempermonkey – This extension advertises itself as the world's most popular user-script manager! It allows you to manage and edit your user-scripts and enable / disable your user-scripts with just two clicks.

 Microsoft Personal Shopping Assistant – It automatically remembers all your browsed products and gives you price change alerts for such saved items.

Turn Off the Lights for Microsoft Edge – It allows you to fade the light of Edge, so imitating the cinema atmosphere when playing videos.

Like me, you might have installed one of the above extensions, then changed your mind and now you want to remove it from your device. Luckily, this is easy to do. Tap or click the **Menu** button at the top-right of the screen in **Microsoft Edge**, also shown here, to display the **Menu** ··· screen. All the extensions you downloaded and activated are listed at the top of the screen, one of which is shown here in Fig. 6.5.

Next, touch and hold or right-click the extension you want to remove and select **Manage** from the drop-down menu, to display the screen in Fig. 6.6 on the next page.

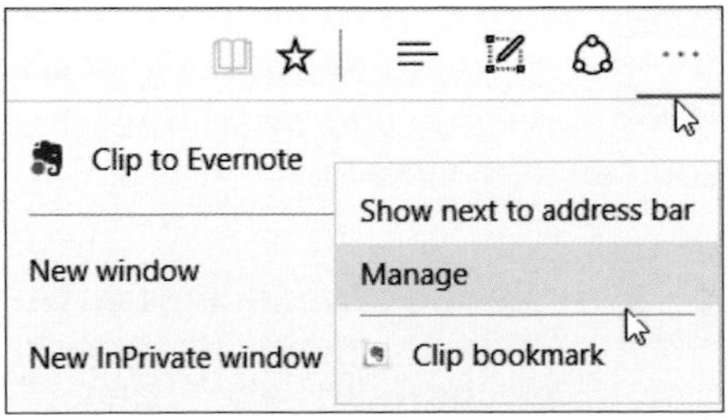

Fig. 6.5 Managing Extensions.

Uninstalling Edge Extensions

On this screen and for this particular extension, you are reminded first what it does and are given the option to turn it off, if so you wished, or to **Uninstall** it. All you have to do is press the button pointed to in Fig. 6.6 for the extension to be removed from your device.

> « Evernote Web Clipper   ⊷
>
> About
> Use the Evernote extension to save things you see on the
> web into your Evernote account.
>
> Rate and review
>
> Version: 6.9.2.0
> Installed: 01/11/2016
>
> This extension is allowed to:
> • Read and change your cookies
> • See the websites you visit
> • Read and change content on websites you visit
>
> Evernote Web Clipper
>
> ⬤◯ On
>
> Show button next to the address bar
>
> ◉◯ Off
>
> [Options]
>
> [Uninstall]

Fig. 6.6 Uninstalling Extensions.

As you can see, from the list of the presently available extensions for **Microsoft Edge**, some have the same functionality, so it might be a good idea to choose what is useful to you and not be afraid to remove later what doesn't work for you.

Other Microsoft Edge Changes

There a lot of improvements made to **Edge**, some behind the scenes, like better navigation with a keyboard, better support for address bar suggestions and lots of bug fixes.

Other more visible improvements help to make your daily browsing experience easier and more enjoyable, such as:

• Better support for PDF files (but see Chapter 3 page 30).

• The new **Microsoft Edge** browser now determines whether **Flash** content is important to a Web page. If it is, like news videos, they are allowed to play, but if they are ads, they are blocked (though you can still choose to play them manually if you so wish).

In addition, it might help if you right-click an unwanted advert to get **Adobe Flash Help** and select **Global Settings** from the displayed context menu, as shown in Fig. 6.7.

This opens the **Flash Player Help** screen shown in Fig. 6,8 below from which you can choose to change **Global Privacy Settings** from the

| Settings... |
| Global Settings... |
| Check for Updates... |
| About Adobe Flash Player 23.0.0.205... |

Fig. 6.7 The Right-click Context Menu of an Ad.

displayed panel. The **Settings Manager** on the screen is not an image, but an actual **Settings Manager**, so whatever changes you make here, they take effect on **Adobe Flash Player**.

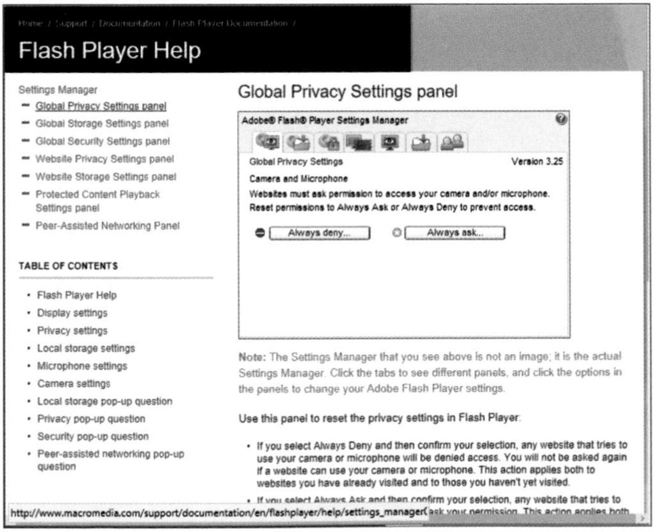

Fig. 6.8 The Adobe Flash Player Settings Manager.

- You can now create pinned tabs in **Microsoft Edge**. Simply right-click any tab and choose **Pin**, to have your most used sites and Web apps available, just by clicking on their pinned tab, as shown in Fig. 6.9 for three pinned sites.

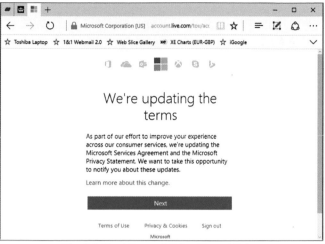

Fig. 6.9 The Microsoft Edge Pinned Tabs.

- Having copied a link to the clipboard, you can now right-click it in the address bar and select **Paste and go** from the displayed context menu to navigate to the new site, as shown in Fig. 6.10.

Fig. 6.10 The Paste and Go Context Menu.

- You can now import into **Microsoft Edge**, your **Favourites** from **Firefox** in addition to **Internet Explorer** and **Chrome**. Such imported **Favourites** will be imported into a separate folder so as not to mix them up with your existing ones.

On the browser where your favourites are:

1. Open the browser
2. Go to **File**, **Import and export**
3. Select to **Export** to a file
4. Tick the **Favourites** option and press **Next**
5. Tap or click **Export** to export your favourites to an **html** file.

On **Microsoft Edge**:

1. Tap or click the **More** button
2. Select **Settings** from the drop-down menu
3. Tap or click the **View favourites settings**
4. Tick the browser holding your favourites
5. Tap or click the **Import** button.

- **Microsoft Edge** now supports **Notifications** for updates from open Websites such as **WhatsApp** and **Skype**.

- You can now navigate using a finger to swipe left or right on a touch-sensitive screen device, to go to the next or previous page in your history, as shown below. The circle under 'A safe place' shows the position of my finger on the screen.

Fig. 6.11 Moving from Page to Page in History.

- Touch and hold or right-click on any picture on the Web and select **Ask Cortana** on the displayed context menu to obtain information on that picture as shown in Fig. 6.12.

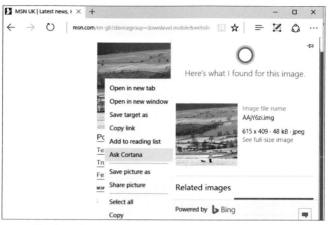

Fig. 6.12 Getting Information on a Picture on the Web.

However, most of the time (to my experience), related information on some pictures is not reliable.

- You can now drag and drop folders kept on cloud sites like **OneDrive**, **Google Drive** and **Dropbox**, directly into **Microsoft Edge**.

But having said that, I was unable to replicate this using either **OneDrive** or **Dropbox**. However, it certainly works fine when using **Internet Explorer** instead of **Microsoft Edge**!

******

I hope that I have given enough information in the chapter on what **Microsoft Edge** can do, so that you can now start using it with confidence. Enjoy and good luck!

******

7

Ink, Dark Theme & Tablet Mode

There are a few extra improvements That come with **Windows 10 Anniversary Update**. Amongst the many such improvements, I discuss a few in this chapter that might be of interest to you.

Windows Ink

To activate **Windows Ink**, left-click an empty area on the **Taskbar** to display the context menu shown in Fig. 7.1, then click the **Show Windows Ink Workspace button**.

This action places the button shown here on the **System Tray**. Clicking this button, displays the **Windows Ink Workspace** shown in Fig. 7.2 on the next page.

Toolbars	>
Cortana	>
✓ Show Task View button	
Show Windows Ink Workspace button	
✓ Show touch keyboard button	
Cascade windows	
Show windows stacked	
Show windows side by side	
Show the desktop	
Task Manager	
Lock the taskbar	
⚙ Settings	

Fig. 7.1 The Context Taskbar Menu Screen.

Sticky Notes

Fig. 7.2 The Windows Ink Workspace.

Now, clicking on the area labelled **Sticky Notes**, displays a sticky note, as shown in Fig. 7.3, ready to type something on it.

Fig. 7.3 A Sticky Note.

You can add another sticky note by clicking the plus (**+**) sign, delete it by clicking the bin (🗑) or change its colour by clicking the **More (...)** button.

This last action displays the screen shown here, but superimposed on the sticky note itself.

The Sketchpad

Clicking the **Sketchpad** area in Fig. 7.2 above displays an enlarged picture of the **Sketchpad**, but with a row or editing tools, as shown here.

Needless to say, you need an appropriate device that allows a pen or stylus to be used on it before you can use this facility. You would also need a pen or stylus to take full advantage.

The Sketch Screen

If you don't have an appropriate device on which a pen or stylus can be used, but you have a PC with a touch sensitive screen, you can use your finger on the **Sketch screen**. This can be displayed by clicking the area with the same name on the screen in Fig. 7.2 shown on the previous page, which opens the screen in Fig. 7.4 below.

Fig. 7.4 The Sketch Screen With its Own Toolbar.

I suggest you spend sometime here to examine the various editing tools on the **Toolbar** at the top of the screen.

Finally, at the bottom of the **Windows Ink Workspace** (Fig. 7.2 on the previous page), you see information on **Recently used** apps and below that of **Suggested** apps that you might like to obtain.

The Dark Theme

Windows 10 Anniversary Update now comes with the ability to change the default white colour of various apps to a dark colour that is friendlier on the eyes.

To achieve this, go to **Start**, then click on **Settings** and on the displayed screen, shown in Fig. 7.5, select the **Personalisation** option, pointed to below.

Fig. 7.5 The Settings Screen With Personalisation Option Selected.

This displays the **Personalisation** screen and selecting the **Colours** option, opens the screen shown in Fig. 7.6 on the next page. To see the bottom half of this screen, you'll have to scroll down. At the very bottom you'll find two options; **Light** (the default) and **Dark**. These options dictate how the background of some apps will display.

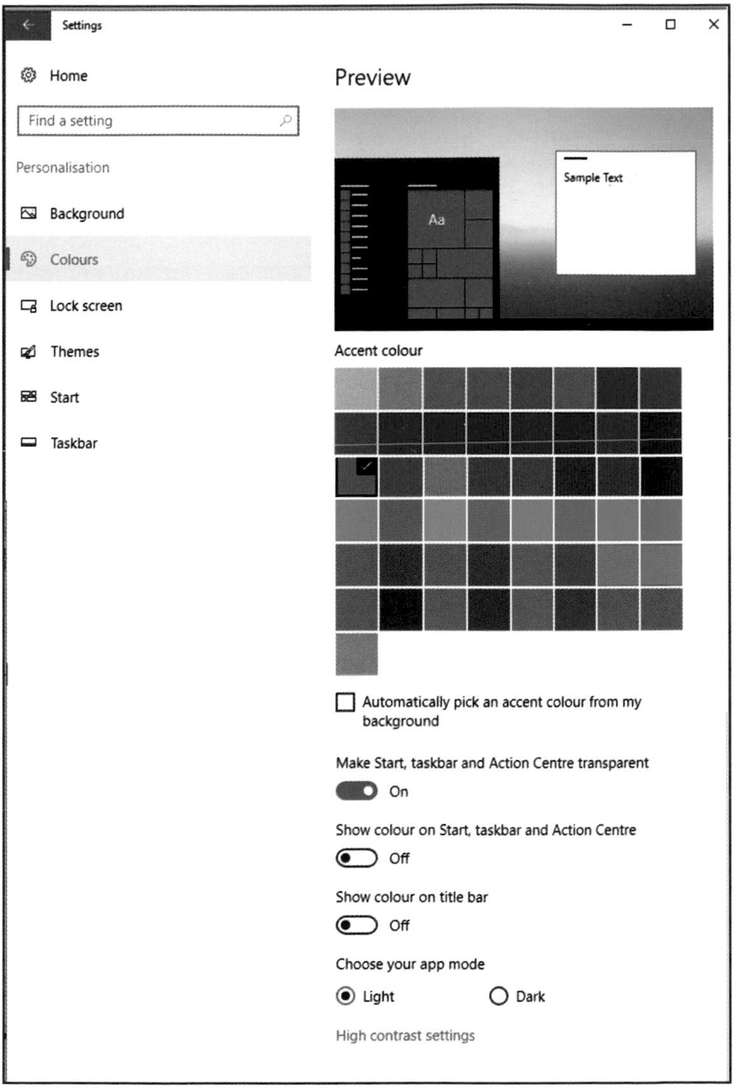

Fig. 7.6 The Light and Dark Colours Personalisation Options.

To test this, select the **Dark** option which has the effect of turning the **Settings** screen from a white background with black writing to a black background with white writing.

However, not all apps respond to this background reversal. For example, **File Explorer**, **Microsoft Edge**, **Control Panel**, **Word**, **Excel**, **News** (to mention but a few) don't change their background colour, while the **Start** menu, **Action Centre**, **Settings**, **Calculator**, **Calendar**, **Alarms and Clocks** (also to mention but a few) do change their background to dark.

In Fig. 7.7, I show the **Calendar** screen in **Dark app mode**.

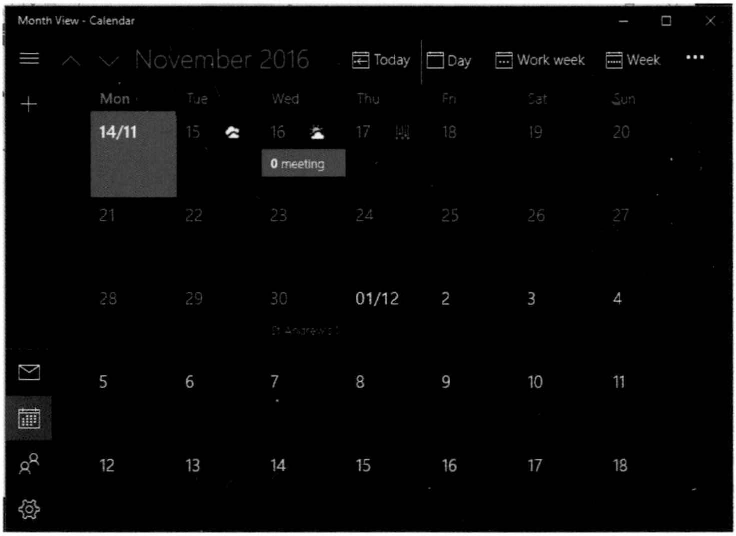

Fig. 7.7 The Calendar Screen in Dark App Mode.

I am sure one can find several reasons for this background reversal option, for example you might have the urge to consult your **Calendar** whilst in bed and you don't want to disturb your partner!

Personally, I prefer to read a book in **Dark** mode, rather than consult my **Calendar** in such a situation, but I am sure there is a better reason for such screen reversal, especially for only selected apps.

Tablet Mode

To place your system in **Tablet Mode**, tap or click on **Notifications** and then tap or click the **Tablet mode** option pointed to in Fig. 7.8.

This displays a full-screen **Pinned tiles** option, but you have a choice of displaying these in **All apps** list, as shown in Fig. 7.9 below.

Fig. 7.8 The Action Centre's Options.

Fig. 7.9 The All Apps List in Tablet Mode.

You can also choose to hide the **Taskbar** whilst in **Tablet mode**, by going to **Settings**, **Personalisation**, selecting the **Taskbar** option, as shown in Fig. 7.10 and turning **On** the **Automatically hide taskbar in tablet mode** switch.

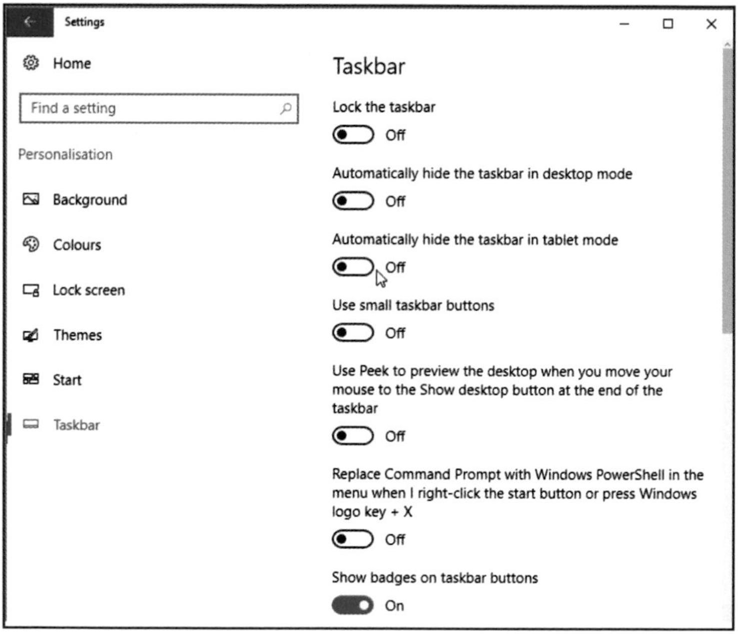

Fig. 7.10 The Taskbar Option of the Personalisation Screen.

Finally, while you have the **Personalisation** screen open, shown in Fig. 7.10 above, tap or click the **Lock screen** option on the left of the screen, to display the screen in Fig. 7.11 shown on the next page.

On this last screen, change the **Background** option from **Windows spotlight** to either **Picture** or **Slideshow**. This will disable **Lock Screen Ads**.

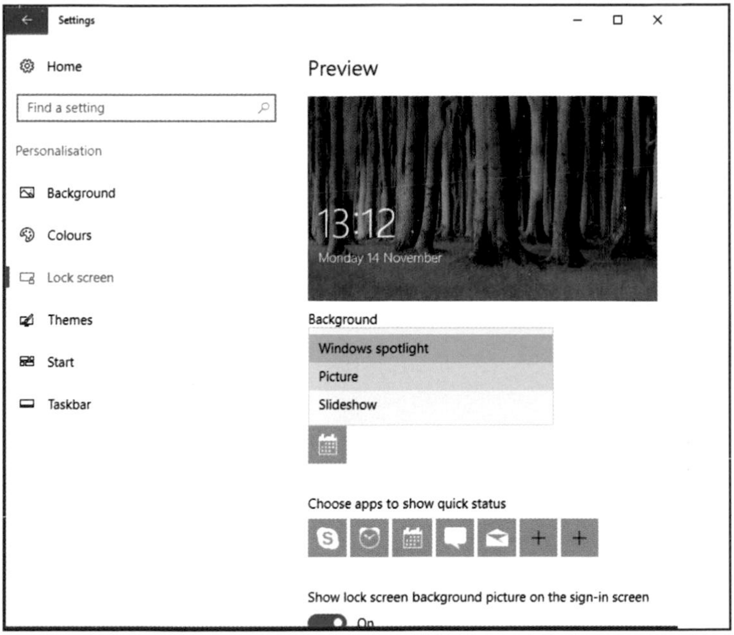

Fig. 7.11 Changing the Background of the Lock Screen.

If you choose **Picture**, you are asked to choose a picture from the ones displayed, as shown in Fig. 7.12, or you can **Browse** to select your own picture.

If you select **Slideshow** for the **Background**, you are then asked to choose a picture folder.

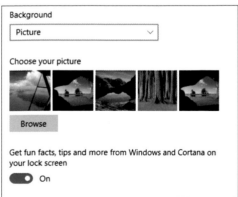

Fig. 7.12 Choosing a Lock Screen Picture.

* * * * * *

Obviously there are a lot more improvements included in the **Anniversary Update**, some obvious, others not so obvious, but hopefully, I have covered the main ones with sufficient detail for you to go ahead and be confident enough to enjoy and gain the benefits from this new version of **Windows 10**.

* * * * * *

Index

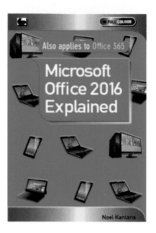

Also available by Noel Kantaris (978 0 85934 762 4)

This book is based on the Home and Business edition of Microsoft's Office 2016 PC-based software. It will also be very useful to Office 365 users, as a large part of this subscription and cloud-based package is based on Office 2016.

The book covers Word, Outlook, Excel, PowerPoint and OneNote all of which can be used on Desktop, Laptop and Tablet devices with mouse or touch-screen control.

Each application within the 'Home and Business' edition of Office 2016: Word, Excel, PowerPoint, OneNote and Outlook is introduced with sufficient detail to get you working. No prior knowledge of these applications is assumed and easy-to-follow hands-on examples are included that should help you get-to-grips with Office 2016 quickly and easily.